To Dad.
Happy Birthday 1983

Jean & Gordon.

On the Rails

Sidney Weighell

On the Rails

With an appreciation by Robert Taylor

ORBIS PUBLISHING · LONDON

Contents

A selection of photographs appears between pages 96 and 97

To my father and grandfather,
who made it possible for me to say with pride: I am a
third-generation railwayman, trade unionist
and Socialist

To my mother,
sisters Elma and Brenda and my brother Maurice for
their help and understanding when they felt the public
pressure during the turbulent times of my period as a
trade union leader

To my son Anthony,
who despite the stress and strain of going through three
universities to gain his PhD found time to find the best
trout streams on which we could fish together and
helped to ease the pressures of work

To all those friends
both in and out of the trade union and Labour
movements who shared a common purpose

And to my wife Joan,
who was always there in times of crisis to pull up the
drawbridge and shut out the world, and who thought I
would never finish this book

Acknowledgements
I am most grateful to Robert Taylor and
Charlie Turnock, without whose help this book would
not have been possible

An Appreciation by Robert Taylor

Sidney Weighell should be remembered as one of the outstanding trade union leaders of his generation. Articulate, forceful, brave and true to his democratic Socialist beliefs, he gave invaluable service to the National Union of Railwaymen and the wider Labour movement. He has always been a combative, spiky character and he has made plenty of political enemies through his belligerent, plain-speaking oratory and his razor-sharp mind. To a great extent, Sidney Weighell fought his many battles on his own and he took no prisoners. In a movement that thrives on camaraderie and factionalism, he tended to stand apart. But even his bitterest opponents could not deny the fierceness of his integrity and the skill with which he fought his corner against all comers.

There are very few trade union leaders in Britain at any time who can think and act on the problems of the Labour movement beyond the narrow limitations of their own unions. Sidney Weighell was one of those exceptions. His passionate defence of a voluntary incomes policy in a planned economy was combined with a visionary outlook of what the Trades Union Congress could achieve in increased influence and power in Britain if its members would provide it with much more centralized authority. His dream is of a united and strong trade union movement based on the principles of industrial unionism on the West German model, a vision not shared by many other union leaders, who continue to value the sectionalism and independence of our present structure and dislike notions of a wider solidarity in the interests of organized labour. Sidney Weighell's ideas fly in the face of TUC traditions, though they are certainly none the worse for that.

In the Labour Party again he fought the good fight without many followers. Sidney Weighell was not a bully with a block vote. Indeed, he found it hard to wheel and deal, intrigue and manipulate, and it is ironic that his resignation came from a tactical switch in NUR preferences at the 1982 Labour Party conference which, in many people's view, was well justified. Unlike many other union leaders, Sidney Weighell did not operate by way of alliances made in smoke-filled rooms.

Nor did he opt for a quiet life in the face of the mounting, incontrovertible evidence of far-Left infiltration into Labour's ranks. Too many union leaders did little and said nothing about what was going on and they were belated in their desperate efforts to save the party from a lurch into extremism. Sidney Weighell was never prepared to equivocate or compromise his deeply-held principles and he went down with all guns blazing in the debates, where he was out-fought not by the intelligence of the counter-arguments used against him but by the sheer weight of the orchestrated block votes.

Sidney Weighell was often accused of being an autocrat, of trying to turn the National Union of Railwaymen into a personal tyranny. This was always a complete falsehood. It is true that he refused to play the role of the time-server, like so many union leaders prefer to do when they reach the top of their unions late in life with no energy or ideas left to fight for. He believed in giving a sense of direction to his members. He had no effective sanctions to impose his will on other people, but he did possess remarkable gifts of language and common sense that could sway an audience in debate to see the wisdom of his point of view.

He has never believed that leadership in a trade union and a belief in democratic self-government were incompatible. Some other union leaders of his generation were content to act as messenger boys, cyphers of the views of the small cliques who controlled their union executives. Sidney Weighell left neither friend nor foe in any doubt where he stood on the issues of the day.

Since his resignation many on the hard Left regard Sidney Weighell absurdly as somehow a traitor to the working class. Rewriting Labour history is a full-time preoccupation for some, but this remains a travesty of the truth. Sidney Weighell stands firmly in the broad mainstream of the Labour movement. He believes in the planned economy, in public ownership, in the redistribution of wealth and income, in social justice and equality. From his early days as a railwayman's son in Northallerton he has been soaked in the ideals and principles of democratic Socialism.

But perhaps today's Labour party no longer has any room inside it for somebody with his background. Sidney Weighell may well turn out to be one of the last genuinely working-class trade union leaders in Britain. A self-taught man, who left school at fifteen to start work, he came to the Labour movement through the experiences of living and working in the depression of the thirties. The Baptist chapel played a crucial part in his making. He has an understandable contempt for middle-class Socialists, who went to public schools and Oxbridge, and claim to speak for the proletariat. The world of the polytechnocracy, which dominates so much of the Labour Party nowadays, is light years away from the Labourist traditions reflected in his career.

As General Secretary of the NUR from April 1975 until January 1983 Sidney Weighell found himself fighting one battle after another against forces that were much more powerful than perhaps he realized at the time. For eight years he had to lobby again and again for the future of the railway industry against successive governments that tended to see the railways as a drain on public resources rather than a vital national asset that needed massive support to thrive. The railways had few friends in high places. Starved of badly needed investment for new rolling stock, signals and track, British Rail staggered through a seemingly endless crisis of uncertainty and false hopes.

Sidney Weighell was also plagued by persistent and self-destructive conflicts with the train drivers' union, the Associated Society of Locomotive Engineers and Firemen (ASLEF). These weakened union unity in the industry and greatly strengthened the hands of those who wanted to cut back the network and undermine its services. Inside his own union, he faced a growing and formidable threat from the hard Left, who did not disguise their determination to bring him down.

Sidney Weighell has often given the impression that he was an angry and frustrated man, exasperated by the follies of others and impatient with those who advised caution and compromise. His desire to get things done comes through loud and clear. In his own union, in the TUC, in the Labour Party, above all in the crisis-ridden railway industry, he has campaigned actively for radical change.

The British trade union movement always works at its best when it enjoys a sense of coherence and direction, and this can only come from men and women of vision who are not content merely to administer their unions but who want to change the world for the betterment of their members and their country. We too often overlook the crucial impact made by individuals on the history of British trade unionism. There is an understandable distaste for any cult of the personality, but trade unions are not run by rulebooks and filing cabinets, procedures and protocol, anonymous committees and mass conferences. It is complex human beings who have made the Labour movement what it is today.

Sidney Weighell – for all the sneers of his enemies – deserves to be remembered for the positive impact he made on his union, on the TUC and on the Labour party. Today his legacy may look modest and many of the causes he fought for seem doomed or irrelevant in the new harsher world of free collective bargaining and Thatcherism. In the next few years the British trade union movement will have to fight to survive as it sees many of the landmarks of the post-war period – the welfare state, the managed economy, full employment, the industrial consensus – fading away.

In his own union, Sidney Weighell showed how a union's structure could be brought up to date. He believed in harnessing professionalism to the improvement of the conditions of railway workers, and he was quick and efficient in creating the conditions in which professionalism could operate. The new Unity House, the NUR college at Frant, the revitalized NUR parliamentary group, and the streamlining of the administration – all these reforms came in a very short period of time. In his handling of the rail crises of 1980-82 he tried to take a constructive course of action, despite the pressures, motivated by his clear and attractive vision of a new railway system for Britain. But as his story indicates, there were many in government and in other rail unions who were not prepared to modernize the network, trading investment for efficiency.

But in Sidney Weighell's life story, in his actions and in his words, we can find signposts to a more constructive approach to the role of the unions in a modern, interdependent society. His views on the need for discipline and order in trade union affairs may not appeal to some, and his defence of the closed shop may upset the middle-class individualists, who fail to recognize the case for its introduction in the defence of trade union rights. But his sudden departure from the world of the unions leaves a vacuum which will prove hard for anybody to fill. Like him or not, Sidney Weighell brought a fierce integrity, a passionate commitment, a rare idealism to an often grubby, cynical and hypocritical Labour movement.

More than anything else he will be remembered for his persistent determination to expose the contradictions that exist between a belief in Socialism and the practice of free collective bargaining. In doing so, Sidney Weighell exposed the central weakness of British trade unionism for all to see. The tensions that exist today between the immediate needs of trade unionism and the longer-term aspirations of democratic Socialism remain as real and intractable as ever. It would be wrong to suggest that Sidney Weighell found a satisfactory answer in his analysis of that particular trade union 'problem', but at least he asked the crucial question when so few other trade union leaders could be bothered to do so.

If the lessons of his often difficult period as the NUR's thirteenth General Secretary are learned from this book, Sidney Weighell will have made a further contribution to the future of British trade unionism. He himself has quoted Edmund Burke: 'For evil to triumph, it is only necessary for good men to do nothing.' It cannot be said of Sidney Weighell that he did nothing. On the contrary, his dynamic eight years at the head of the NUR have left solid achievements that his detractors cannot take away from him. His story provides a lasting testament to them.

The Making of a Union Leader

I was born on 31 March 1922 in Northallerton, a small, rich Tory town in a beautiful part of the North Riding of Yorkshire. My mother wanted me to be called Sydney in memory of the building of the Sydney harbour bridge in Australia. At the time the nearby Teesside firm of Dorman Long had just won the contract to build it, and this was a great event in the North-East. However, the Registrar of Births refused to register my name with a y, insisting I should be named Sidney. Nevertheless, my mother always spelt my name as she had chosen.

I grew up in a family dominated by the railways. My grandfather William had been a guard and founder member in 1883 of the Northallerton branch of the old Amalgamated Society of Railway Servants. My father Tom was a signalman, who at the age of sixteen took part in the 1911 strike for recognition. Both men had the same attitude to being railwaymen. They took a pride in their job, believing in a fair day's work for a fair day's pay. They gave good service to the railways and they expected to receive the same treatment from the railway company in return.

My grandfather was active in trade union work, becoming the local union branch treasurer. In his spare time he helped to found the Co-operative store in the town, and he made up the orders and delivered them to customers.

Father was more articulate. In fact he was a highly effective speaker on public platforms. He had learned his oratorical skills as a lay preacher at the Baptist chapel before the First World War, although when he came back from fighting in the trenches as a sergeant he never preached again. Oddly, he never spoke about his war experiences. He eventually became Chairman of the Bench in Northallerton, a pillar of the community.

Father was a tremendous influence on my life and gave me invaluable advice. 'We'll never change this world just by preaching about it,' he used to say to me. 'You've got to do something about it yourself.' He held a number of important offices in the union, including sitting on the National Executive, and was awarded both the BEM and the MBE for public service. I looked up to him throughout his life. Although we had our occasional differences, he always took a keen interest in my career in the union.

My mother's family, the Hardistys, were business people in the town. Her father was a greengrocer and a stalwart of the Baptist chapel – I can still remember him dressed up in his special constable's uniform, complete with bowler hat and truncheon. Behind his shop was a warehouse full of fruit and confectionery. He never forbade us from going in there and eating what we liked, for he knew we would soon get sick of it. He was successful in business and used to drive around proudly in a bull-nosed Morris, in which he often took my brother Maurice, my two sisters Elma and Brenda and myself on rides over the moors around Northallerton.

We never went short of food at home. We were well fed and well clothed. There were many things we couldn't buy, but our home was always comfortable at a time when unemployment was very high in the North-East and poverty much more widespread than it is today. There was not an excessive discipline in our house at 12 Arncliffe Terrace, but discipline there was when my father was about.

I was an ordinary boy, reading comics like the *Wizard* and the *Hotspur* and swapping them around like kids still do. I went to the local Church of England school, but I never really showed much interest and my father used to complain that I didn't try. I never got over the hurdle of the eleven-plus examination to go to the grammar school.

I preferred playing football and cricket or walking in the countryside to doing homework. But I did go to Sunday school until I was thirteen, and that left a lasting impression on me. I remember having to learn verses from the Psalms by heart. Although I didn't attend chapel after my early teens, every Sunday evening hymns from the BBC service on the radio would fill our house with song. Father knew all the best hymns word for word. Today when I hear

13

hymns sung on the television service on Sunday nights they bring a lump to my throat. Mother is still chapel organist.

Our house was a beacon of light for people in trouble in North-allerton. My father virtually ran the union single-handed as well as the local Labour Party at election times. Our front room became a sort of citizen's advice bureau and social security office. Everybody seemed to know our house was the place to go to if you lost your job or your home or needed advice.

I began to help father with his union work from a very early age. I used to address envelopes and pack circulars for the members, reading their names off from the union collector's slips of paper for entry into the branch contribution book. From time to time I was sent off to collect trade union contributions from members in the town.

We were a light-hearted family and I didn't grind my way to Socialism, though there were plenty of trade union and Socialist books round the house. My beliefs came from those principles of tolerance, fairness and decency which I learned at home and which are the human values that lie deep in working-class communities.

I've never believed that Socialists born with silver spoons in their mouths or disillusioned intellectuals would lead us to the promised land. It is the ordinary men and women who want to put society right who will show the way forward.

It was in my early teens that I first became aware of the inequalities and unfairness of life for many people, seeing how the problems that were disclosed in our house made my parents angry. But I soon learned too that this anger at injustice had to be turned into constructive action. We had to change society by showing the better way by our example, by reason and sound argument and not with a pickaxe handle.

A man once came to our house with a dismissal notice he had got from the railway. My father knew all about seniority and 'first in, first out' and he could see straight away that the notice wasn't meant for that fellow, but for someone else. So he said to him: 'That's not yours. There's been a mistake.'

But the man replied: 'I don't give a toss whose it is as long as it's not mine.' My father, who believed not only in fairness, but in caring what happens to others, gave him hell for saying that, telling him that as a union member he ought to be concerned about his fellow workers.

I left school at the age of fifteen in 1937 and became an apprentice motor mechanic. The following year I took an apprenticeship at the road motor engineering depot of the London and North Eastern Railway company at Thirsk. I didn't really like the idea of going to work. There was a lazy streak in me, and working at Thirsk meant getting up very early every morning and travelling eight miles.

In January 1940 I was transferred to the locomotive department in Northallerton as a fireman. The war had started four months earlier and there was already an acute shortage of railway staff, so that overtime working became excessive. There were long, hard hours of shiftwork, so that one winter during the war I hardly ever saw the daylight. Then in 1943 I became a qualified engine driver.

My brother Maurice also made his life on the railways, becoming a train driver as well on Teesside. He was active in the union for some years at local level and he could have gone a long way in the movement if he had wished.

To start with I was not very active in the union, but the grind of shiftwork was getting me down and I began complaining about the working arrangements to my father. 'Don't complain to me,' he replied. 'If there are things that you believe are wrong, then do something about it yourself.' So I started going to union branch meetings. They were held every three weeks in the Durham Ox hotel. At first I went along and said nothing, but gradually I plucked up courage to have my say. If you said anything stupid, the older men were quick to jump on you. They were rough and tough but they were also fair-minded. You had to work to earn your spurs with them.

After a year I decided to stand for election to the local departmental committee. I remember going to the branch for eight people to sign my nomination papers. To my great surprise, I was elected. At the tender age of twenty I was launched on my trade union career.

The committee made me their secretary. It was my job to look after the branch's business and argue the union case before local management. You were given time off to deal with problems but there was no pay for this work. In representing the men, if you showed any signs of weakness, you'd had it. They gave no quarter and they expected none. You had to know more and show you were better than them if you wanted to survive.

Meetings of the union in those days attracted more men than they do now. There was fierce competition from the branches to send delegates to district council level. I attended the Leeds and

York district council of the union from the Northallerton branch. The heavy demands of union work at that time were made easier by being single, as I then still was. I had to go to meetings at my own expense.

I recall telling my father that the going was so rough that I wouldn't go to any more of those area conferences again. He told me that this was what the trade union movement was all about. It was a tough movement because it was concerned with working life, and that was tough. I would find that it would become even more difficult if I continued to play an active part in the union. He said that the best way to survive and cope was to equip yourself. Make sure you know what you're talking about when you get on your feet to speak and don't be up and down like a jack-in-the-box. It was far better to make one telling speech than make half a dozen about nothing. You would always find people would drop on you like a ton of bricks if you let them – that was the trade union movement.

I made a big effort to prepare myself. I took correspondence courses with the National Council of Labour Colleges, learning about chairmanship, statistics and mathematics, and also attended summer schools held by the NCLC and the Labour Party.

People often ask me why I joined the NUR rather than ASLEF, which I could have done as an engine driver. When, during the period of a few years working at Darlington, the local chairman of ASLEF had asked me why I wanted to stay in the NUR, he had told me: 'We drivers are a craft and not like other railway workers.' But I disagreed. I thought then and always have that footplatemen are no better and no worse than other railway workers. They have no right to think they are an élite who can look down on the rest. So I became a convinced industrial unionist at an early age. All the ASLEF talk about special treatment and higher status contradicted everything I had been taught at home and in the chapel about the strong helping the weak and everybody working together.

Drivers could be real autocrats. But when I was a fireman I had a simple reply when they tried to order me about. I told them if I stopped shovelling coal into the engine there wouldn't be any steam and the train wouldn't move. I believe everybody, not just the drivers, is needed to make the railways work.

At the same time as I began to take an active part in NUR work, I was also a keen footballer. In 1945 the amateur club of West Auckland, in the Northern League, asked me to play for them as an inside left. I agreed and took time off work to play. When I was attending union conferences in Leeds and York at that time, a car used to pick me up at one o'clock on Saturdays and drive me up to the games in the North-East. Sunderland, Newcastle and Sheffield United all invited me for trials, and on 12 October 1945 I signed for Sunderland for a fee of £10.

I played for two seasons alongside the lads at Roker Park in the reserve team. With the legendary Reich Carter in the first team, I didn't stand much chance of getting into that but I got a basic £3 a game, plus a bonus if we won, on top of my £3 a week on the railways. I was so well off that I could even afford to run a second-hand MG sports car!

Playing football posed a problem for me then because I was representing men at the depot, and also there was a staff shortage. I had an example to set so I used to switch turns of duty rather than take time off. Some Saturday nights I had to work 10 pm turns so that I could play football in the afternoon. I had never intended to give up my job on the railways, as a footballer's future is always very questionable: you can only last until you get to about thirty, even at the very top.

The North-East produces high-quality footballers. In those days a First Division match could regularly attract crowds of 50,000. As many as 15,000 would turn up to watch the Sunderland second team. Lads would play for nothing just to get a Sunderland jersey on their backs. I enjoyed the keen competition and the experience of playing with top players, but after the 1947 season I left Sunderland and went back to playing locally. I continued playing football up to my first election to the union's National Executive Committee in 1953.

By the time I signed with Sunderland I was becoming active in the wider Labour movement. In 1945 I joined the Labour Party and became a member of the local trades council, where I represented the union. I was seen by some as a disruptive influence and a bit of a left-winger. I used to take up issues with the local council, but they ignored my letters. My behaviour upset some of the staider types on the trades council and they expelled me for bringing politics into the council. The TUC sent Vic Feather up to Northallerton to sort out the row, but I was banned from the trades council for the period of a year.

In those days I had a mild aspiration to follow a political career inside the Labour Party, and submitted my name for List B of the party as a potential parliamentary candidate. In 1947 I took on the job of agent in the Richmond constituency because nobody else would do it. In such a rock-solid Conservative seat, held by Sir Thomas Dugdale, it was heartbreaking work. Labour never stood a chance there. I did a lot of travelling around speaking to stone walls and black-faced sheep.

It was maddening to go round and see the pretty farmworkers' cottages with roses climbing round the door. Inside the floor was just earth, but they had 'Vote Conservative' stickers in their windows. Of course, I realized they were afraid to do anything else because these were tied cottages and the employer owned the roof over the occupants' heads.

I remained Labour agent through the 1950 and 1951 general elections but I decided that my future lay with the union rather than the party. It was father who told me to concentrate on the NUR and drop the political activity.

In 1947 I was elected as the youngest delegate to attend the union's annual conference in Ayr, representing the Teesside and North Yorkshire area – perhaps I won on the first ballot because the members thought they were voting for my father! But in the next year I went round every branch in the area to meet the members. The competition to be a delegate at Conference was always keen in those days and I had to beat men from the powerful Teesside block.

The power of the Parliament of the union became clear to me in my first year as a delegate. But I could also see the influence the platform could exert on the delegates, especially the General Secretary, who always made sure he was well briefed on the major issues. The full-time officers in the union who were the most successful were also the most experienced and had established reputations for fair dealing and knowing their subject inside out. In my opinion, speaking with conviction was also important in winning support from the conference delegates. A new General Secretary or an Assistant General Secretary always had the most difficult time to establish themselves, but if they were capable they eventually put that right.

I was not consciously seeking out a powerful position in the union, but as I became more and more interested and active I was also aware that at whatever level I was operating it was always somewhere else that the real decisions were made.

The Northallerton branch nominated me for a job as union

divisional officer at the age of twenty-five. I took the tests set by the union to see what was required on that first occasion, and I failed on the subject of branch finance. But I sat the examinations again and came out top. Now I was free from any pressure about seeking office in the union. Having that qualification under my belt I could then concentrate on other issues.

In my twenties I was active at some time in every level of the union's organization. I was a young delegate to no less than four annual conferences and eight special ones during those years. In 1953 I was elected to be a member of the union's Executive Committee at the tender age of thirty-one. It takes at least a year to find out how the Executive works, wading through volumes of paper and attending top-level meetings. In the NUR Executive members have a full-time job to do for the union and they are away from their work on the railways for three-year stretches, not being allowed to stand again for a consecutive three-year stint.

However, after only a year on the Executive I was elected a full-time divisional officer, and took over in June 1954. This meant moving south permanently to work at the union's headquarters in London's Euston Road. By then I had also married Margaret, a local Northallerton girl two years younger than me, and we had two small children. We set up home in St Albans just north of the capital.

I had a background as good as any to understand how the union worked, and at only thirty-two I was part of the NUR administration. But without my father's wealth of experience and knowledge I very much doubt whether I could have made such a rapid move up the union hierarchy.

Yet hardly had we settled into the new life when it was destroyed in one terrible moment. On 21 December 1956 I was motoring up to Northallerton with my wife and two children for Christmas, when I was involved in a head-on crash at Newark railway bridge. My wife and my four-year-old daughter Jennifer were killed, though my son Anthony was saved. I escaped with a badly broken jaw. I spent three months in Sheffield Royal Hospital. The first thing I saw when I recovered consciousness was a file of angels passing by the foot of my bed. In fact they were nurses performing some Christmas festivities. My jaws were locked together with wire through the top and the bottom gum so that I could not open my mouth. It slowly dawned on me what had happened. A nurse told me gently that only my son and myself had survived the accident.

After I left hospital I went to live first with my parents in Northallerton and then on the poultry farm of my father-in-law, five miles away, where I began to recover both mentally and physically. I stayed there for some months, walking on the moors, trout fishing and working on the farm. I even thought about quitting the union for good. Then watching my young son one day, it dawned on me that at thirty-four I had a long time to go and a boy to raise.

I went back to Northallerton, took up golf to help my recovery and renewed contact with the local people. Gradually I began working my way back into my union job. The General Secretary – Jim Campbell – agreed that I should assist the Newcastle-based divisional officer on the days that I felt able to work.

My first problem was to get back into a car driving seat after what had happened. With my father's help and the use of his car, I finally started to drive myself again. But even today if my second wife or son are going on a car journey without me and if they become overdue I get anxious.

But mental readjustment was the greatest difficulty I had to cope with. It really took me five years to recover fully, if you ever do get over such an experience. The troubles I had to face in future years had always to be measured against those dark times after the car crash. Every time I travel by car on the A1 I pass the railway bridge at Newark where the accident happened. Trying to recover was made more difficult by having to appear at the coroner's court and the court in which the unfortunate man who had crashed head-on into me was charged with dangerous driving. He had also lost his wife who was pregnant. Then there was a further appearance in the civil court dealing with the claim for damages when I had to listen to the judge valuing the loss of my wife and daughter. After each of these court appearances it took several days for me to recover, because all the details of the crash had to be repeated.

That was truly a bleak period of my life, but I have often thought of how devastating that Christmas of 1956 must have been for both families. A further incident really rocked me. Visiting the garage outside Newark to collect some personal items from the wrecked car, I opened the door to see Christmas presents scattered over the floor and other personal items covered in blood. I felt as if somebody had hit me with a club.

Late in 1957 I had to return to Sheffield hospital for a minor operation on my jaw. I stayed overnight after the operation, and had just recovered from the anaesthetic when I was told that the union's General Secretary, Jim Campbell, and the President, Tom Hollywood, had been killed on a visit to Russia. Campbell had paid me a visit earlier in the year in hospital and he was a friend of my father's, serving with him on the NUR Executive.

At the end of the year I went back to London and head office where I took on the job of relief divisional officer. This meant a lot of travelling and as my son was in Northallerton with his grand-parents, I saw no point in applying for a settled post in one of the major centres where the divisional officers are located.

I was a relief officer for seven years and as a result I became known to every branch secretary and active union member in the country. This was to be a considerable advantage for me when later I stood for election to the Assistant General Secretary's position.

In November 1959 I remarried. I had met Joan in Manchester, where she was a market researcher. Joan learned about the Labour and trade union movement after we met. She used to travel extensively with me in my union work, but she pulled up the drawbridge when I got home and the media tried to intrude into our private lives. However it became difficult in later years to keep the pressure out of the house.

I was concerned about the effects of the car crash on my young son Anthony, but happily he emerged unscathed. After leaving grammar school, he went to Keele University where he took an honours degree in geology in 1976. Four years later he achieved a PhD at the University of Wales in Aberystwyth and he now has a job with Britoil in Glasgow.

In 1965 I was elected an Assistant General Secretary of the NUR and four years later I became Senior AGS, deputizing for Sidney Greene, the General Secretary, whenever the need arose. I spent a decade at our headquarters at Unity House in what for much of the time was virtually the number two post and over that period I came to familiarize myself with a wide range of different responsibili-ties, which stood me in good stead in my own later years as General Secretary.

I found Sidney Greene a difficult man to understand. He said very little and he kept himself to himself. The union tended to drift along during his long period as General Secretary, keeping a low profile towards the outside world. But as the years rolled by Greene, with his TUC activities taking up much of his time, gave me more and more work, so I was not kept away from the action to stagnate in the backroom, as did happen to men in my position in other unions and still does.

The Labour Party conference in 1966 was the first time I hit the national newspaper headlines. Greene had been called back to London because his mother had just died, so I was left in charge of the NUR delegation. I decided to intervene in the pay debate. The Transport and General Workers' Union (TGWU) General Secretary Frank Cousins had recently resigned from the Labour Government in protest at the incomes policy being enforced at the time, and he attacked the Government's strategy at the conference.

In my maiden speech to the party conference I opposed him and his union for their views. I received a rough ride from many of the delegates who did not like what I had to say. There were shouts of 'Scab' as I criticized Cousins for his demand that there should be work-sharing in the car industry to protect jobs. 'He talks about 10,000 people in a shake-out in the car industry,' I argued. 'Well, 150,000 of our workers have been shaken out.' I wagged my finger at Harry Nicholas, Deputy General Secretary of the TGWU, and declared: 'If he has a car worker who wants a job on the railways in Birmingham I will get him one. He knows why they won't come into our industry ['Because of your union,' delegates shouted], because he has to work a six- or seven-day week.'

'That's your fault,' somebody shouted at me.

'He will have to work for a pay packet that is much lighter,' I added.

'Shame on you!' roared some delegates.

I asked why my union was backing the Government's incomes policy. Some people shouted that we had sold out our members. 'It is because my members are fed up to the teeth of running like hell in order to stand still,' was my reply. No sooner did we negotiate a pay rise for our members, when its value evaporated because of inflation before the extra money reached their wage packets. I said that my members were tired of working in an industry where they could only get a penny piece if they threatened strike action. 'Almost annually we have been on the verge of a national rail stoppage,' I added.

'On the verge?' jeered some delegates.

'The bouquets for the most effective speech in yesterday's big debate were given to Sidney Weighell, forty-four-year-old Assistant General Secretary of the NUR,' wrote Geoffrey Goodman, industrial editor of the *Daily Mirror*. 'Above all the big names of the trade union world this hitherto unknown name suddenly became the universal talking point.' Little did I know that I was going to get the same sort of reception in later years every time I mentioned the subject of incomes policy.

In October 1972 I was elected to the trade union section of Labour's National Executive Committee on behalf of the NUR and I stayed there for three years. I had attended Labour Party conferences in the early 1950s as a constituency delegate. In those days I had been very impressed by Nye Bevan. He was a brilliant speaker and could sway an audience with the force and eloquence of his words. There were major rows inside the party during the earlier period, but I never felt at the time that the loyalty of people to the Labour movement was under any doubt.

My brief stint on the party Executive was a real eye-opener. Often the atmosphere could be difficult, though the extreme Left was not as strong as it became in the late seventies. The different groups used to sit together facing each other across the table at Executive meetings. There was a caucus beforehand on the hard Left to work out their position on every item on the agenda. The Left always stayed to the very end of the meetings and I stayed with them, but decisions were often taken with as few as eight people in attendance.

It was so obvious what was happening that after a year I tabled a resolution to establish the need for a quorum of not less than two-thirds of the Executive for the committee to continue its work. This was finally adopted, but after I left in October 1975 I understand it was modified to less than that figure.

A big battle I do remember vividly is the one we had over whether the party should decide the number of private companies Labour was going to take into public ownership when returned to power. This was held at the Churchill Hotel in London in late 1973. I sat there late into the night, with only about seven others present despite the importance of the matter. A resolution was carried to specify the number twenty-five in the declaration. I voted against this. Harold Wilson told us he would not accept it and later the figure was overturned, but the incident was a good example of what used to happen when few but the hard core of the Left remained at Executive meetings.

I also remember the extraordinary amount of jealousy over protocol on the party Executive. As at the TUC, there is a seniority order for seating on the Labour conference platform. One year

Barbara Castle was due to sit next to the party leader Harold
Wilson but a change in the system was proposed that would have
meant she had to sit elsewhere. Barbara made an enormous fuss
and there was an angry debate about where she should sit, it being
eventually agreed that she would sit beside the leader after all.

In the early seventies Sidney Greene gave me full scope to
organize a major campaign to champion the needs of the railways,
which were again being questioned by our opponents. I decided
that it was vital that the fight for the network must be far more
than just a trade union struggle. Many people might think that we
were simply concerned with job protection and unconcerned about
the wider national needs of the industry, so I thought it was
absolutely vital that we won friends throughout Britain.

In the autumn of 1972, both at the TUC and at the Labour party
conference, I prepared the ground for what I had in mind. At the
Blackpool Labour conference I moved a motion which called for 'an
integrated transport policy' which would 'ensure a larger and
expanding role for the railways' being 'pursued by the next Labour
Government as a matter of extreme urgency'. In my speech I
argued that it made sense in economic terms to have an efficient
and expanding railway system in Britain, and I reminded the
conference that West Germany and Japan were investing between
ten and twenty times more in their railway systems than we were
in ours. 'We have the most overcrowded roads of any nation in the
world,' I said. 'By looking at America we get a preview of what is
about to arrive in Britain, if it has not already arrived. Cities
buried under layers of motorway, polluted by thousands of motor
vehicles, which are pumping out fumes every day and every hour.'

This was no time for pulling punches. I attacked the vested
interests who were hostile to the railways: the oil companies, the
civil engineering firms building roads, and the road haulage
moguls. Nor did I spare the Transport and General Workers'
Union from my remarks. The resolution I was moving meant
shifting freight traffic from the roads to the railways whether by
'direction or incentive' and I was 'not worried which'. It also meant
restrictions on lorries in our towns and cities, and possible bans on
lorries over summer weekends and public holidays. Ray Buckton,
General Secretary of ASLEF, seconded my resolution and it was
carried without opposition.

But I was not prepared to let the matter rest there. In the next
few weeks I worked through the union to win the support of the

NUR Executive for the creation of a new pressure group to champion the railway cause. With the approval of the NUR Executive, I sent out invitations for a meeting to discuss such a body, not merely to the other rail unions but to environmental groups as well.

We had a very good response to our exploratory meeting which was held at Unity House on 13 November 1972. Representatives of more than twenty organizations turned up, including the Civic Trust, Friends of the Earth and the Conservation Society. As a result, we decided to establish a new organization, Transport 2000. Its foundation meeting was held at NUR Head Office on 6 December 1972. I was made the secretary and an office was established to run the campaign for a new deal for the railways.

We held meetings throughout the country, attracting all-party support, including one on 15 March 1973 in the Central Hall, Westminster where Harold Wilson spoke. Transport 2000 did a great deal to combat the pro-road lobby and was a much more positive approach to the issue of public transport than perhaps we had displayed at the time of Beeching's cuts in the early sixties. I will always be grateful to Sidney Greene for giving me the opportunity to play a major role in its launch.

But Greene often threw me into a complex problem at only a moment's notice. In 1968 I was pitched into the deep end in important talks we were holding with the Board at British Rail's training college at Windsor on pay and productivity. Greene told me quite suddenly that he was unable to lead our team because he had a prior engagement overseas with the International Transport Workers' Federation, so he proposed that I should take his place in the talks.

It was a daunting experience to be put in that position with hardly any warning and on such a complicated but important set of negotiations. Fortunately it turned out to be a success. It may not be widely appreciated what we achieved at that time, but after lengthy talks we did manage to make a deal that boosted railway workers' earnings, especially that of the low paid, and linked this to improved efficiencies. I thought we had achieved a miracle in so short a time.

Early in 1975 Sidney Greene retired after seventeen years as General Secretary. I decided to run for the post, and my Northallerton branch nominated me for it. The election was the first held in the NUR on the block vote system in the branches with the single transferable vote. There was, however, no need for any redistribution of the ballot papers, because I won convincingly on the first count.

The result was:

Sidney Weighell	85,553
Frank Cannon	34,855
Russell Tuck	29,476
Charlie Turnock	10,190

There is no transition period into the General Secretary's post in the NUR. Sidney Greene finished work on his last evening and went home, and I arrived the next day and moved into my new office. You are left to sink or swim at the top of the union, but thankfully I was well prepared by my own efforts for the job in hand. After thirty-five years in the union I had reached the top. But now my real troubles were about to begin.

Fighting in the Wages Jungle

The rail pay crisis of 1975

My first major job as General Secretary was to deal with the 1975 pay claim which I had submitted to the Railways Board in February. The negotiations developed into a huge industrial crisis that nearly brought the shutdown of the industry. The trouble stemmed from the widespread collapse of the Social Contract pay guidelines that the TUC had established after the end of Heath's statutory incomes policy in the summer of 1974.

Union leaders had promised to bargain in a responsible way, but during the winter more and more pay deals were made far beyond the rate of inflation, even though the Wilson Government had done so much in its first year of office to meet union demands on other issues. In March 1975 the miners won a 35 per cent wage increase, while the power workers saw their basic rates climb by a massive 51.4 per cent. Clerical staff in the Civil Service were collecting rises of 30 to 35 per cent, and the postmen's pay packet rose by 38.5 per cent. In a radio interview for the BBC on my first afternoon as General Secretary I complained that the TUC General Council should be exerting pressure on those trade unions which were ignoring their responsibilities under the Social Contract. Congress House should have been making the same effort for a united TUC response as it had done so successfully in the fight against the Tories' 1971 Industrial Relations Act.

There was no chance that the National Union of Railwaymen would accept the Board's 'final' offer of 21.2 per cent for our members, when such huge settlements were being made else-

27

where in the public sector and when this would mean an actual reduction in our living standards. Many railwaymen lived next door to miners, and they were not going to tolerate falling so far behind them. 'It is not the objective of railwaymen either to break the Social Contract or to bring the railway service to a heap of twisted metal around their feet,' I wrote to the *Guardian*. 'The NUR firmly supported the Social Contract when it was drawn up. It steered through technological changes and agreed to genuine productivity deals in the past. Both meant manpower reductions unequalled elsewhere except perhaps in the mines.'

Only a few months before the Railways Board and the Government had admitted that railwaymen were entitled to special treatment because their wages had fallen behind, producing serious recruitment problems and staff shortages. Now we were in a situation where my members were being expected to settle for lower wage rises than other workers, which would push them even further down the pay table.

Inevitably the pay issue was sent to the Railway Staffs National Tribunal, the final court of appeal in the complex industrial relations machinery that governs our industry. It was chaired by Lord McCarthy, the Oxford industrial relations academic. I found him a competent, affable arbitrator with a good grasp of the subject, but he was inclined to go into too much detail in his awards, which created real problems for us.

On 5 May I presented the NUR case to the Tribunal. Little did I know that over the next eight years I would appear with our claims before the Tribunal on no fewer than thirty separate occasions. The previous twenty-five references had been spread over forty years. This in a nutshell shows the measure of our growing troubles in the railway industry.

I did not accept then nor at any other time that my members should be denied adequate rates of pay. The 1955 report of a Court of Inquiry into a pay dispute between the Board and my union, chaired by Sir John Cameron, had declared that railwaymen should be no worse off than their colleagues in comparable industries. I quoted Cameron's words at the Tribunal hearing to back the NUR case: 'The nation has provided by statute that there shall be a nationalized system of railway transport, which must therefore be regarded as a public utility of the first importance. Having willed the end, the nation must will the means. This implies that employees of such a national service should receive a fair and adequate wage, and that, in broad terms, the railwayman should be in no worse position than his colleague in a comparable industry.'

At the Tribunal I stressed the strategic importance of the railways for Britain. We moved 73 per cent of the coal consumed in the country, 75 per cent of the coal that went to the power stations, 76.5 per cent of the coal used in coke ovens in the steel industry. These figures spoke for themselves. They illustrated vividly the vital importance of the railways to Britain's heavy industry.

'I live in a very real and practical world and I cannot justify to my Executive Committee and to my members a settlement which would so obviously worsen the relative position of railwaymen,' I explained to the Tribunal. 'The emphasis on the Board's part has been laid almost exclusively on their financial problems and this in turn has caused them to seek the narrowest possible interpretation of the Social Contract at a time when other nationalized industries have been doing the very reverse.'

Such was the militant mood of my Executive that at one stage they even voted by 14 to 9 to stop me going before McCarthy's Tribunal. They pointed out that other workers had acquired massive pay rises without having to go to arbitration to explain their case. The vital question was asked by my Executive: if others could get big increases through negotiation, why should the NUR be forced to take their claim to arbitration? But I believed that our case was so strong that we would get a fair settlement.

In his arbitration judgement McCarthy recommended a 27.5 per cent rise in basic rates for railwaymen; a minimum earnings guarantee of £36.70 a week for low-paid workers; equal pay for women; and further efficiency proposals which would be negotiated to offset rises in fares and subsidies.

But the Tribunal award was not enough. On 2 June the Executive met to discuss it and voted decisively by 21 votes to 3 to call a national strike from 23 June, unless the Railways Board improved the award. They were demanding a 30 per cent wage increase in line with the 'going rate'. In 1970 the minimum rate for railwaymen was 20p a week more than the minimum for surface workers in the coal industry, but by 1974 the coal workers were £6.35 a week ahead and the McCarthy award would have widened the gap to as much as £7.30 after the miners had had their increase. All I really wanted to see was the relative earnings position of my members kept at its existing level, which meant paying a basic railman a weekly rate of £34.65.

However, the Executive of the drivers' union ASLEF voted unanimously to accept the McCarthy award, and so did the white-collar staff union, the Transport and Salaried Staffs Association (TSSA). We were on our own. I wanted to approach the Railways Board again to find out whether they would make improvements in the award before calling a strike, but my Executive wanted to bring matters to a head by immediate action.

I found out from the start that the job of General Secretary can be a very lonely one. I was in my office going over the details of the award to decide the next step when I became aware of the twelve previous General Secretaries peering down at me from their heavy-framed pictures. I didn't like them gazing at me, and besides they darkened the room, so I had them removed from their time-honoured positions to a more suitable place. It later occurred to me that if any of them had been offered a 27.5 per cent rise they would have collapsed.

It was clearly going to be a rough battle, whoever won. I made immediate contact with other trade unions such as the Mineworkers (NUM), the Post Office Workers (UPOW), and the TGWU, asking them for positive support if the strike went ahead. This meant that we expected them to stop any movement of traffic that was switched from rail to road to beat the strike.

The Railways Board insisted that they could not improve the Tribunal's 27.5 per cent award, and it looked as though the strike would go ahead, causing terrible damage to the economy of the country. Then Harold Wilson, the Prime Minister, made a dramatic intervention. I was at home having a bath when he phoned. My wife shouted that Downing Street wanted to speak to me. I thought she was pulling my leg, but I went to the phone with a towel wrapped round me and sure enough Wilson was on the other end. He said he wanted to see me and my President Dave Bowman at six o'clock that evening to discuss what could be done. I agreed at once. None of us wanted to see the strike start. I have always regarded calling a strike as a last resort and a failure on the part of the negotiators. In my experience you never win a strike: all that happens is that more traffic and jobs are lost. But there are times when you may have no choice.

Wilson said he wanted a private chat with us, but when I walked up Whitehall from Westminster tube station and into Downing Street the men from the media were all there waiting for me. The flashbulbs popped as I went through the front door with Bowman.

The Prime Minister asked us to summon our Executive back to London for the following day for a further meeting with him.

It was not my first visit to Downing Street, for in previous pay disputes we had often ended up meeting the Prime Minister of the day, but previous visits had been formal and arranged through proper channels. In fact, we had almost begun to view a visit as a stage in our negotiating machinery. On one notable occasion in 1958 Harold Macmillan had reminded the NUR committee of the sacrifices made on the Western Front in the First World War, and had appealed to their sense of patriotism to cause them to drop their threat of a strike!

The 1975 meeting came immediately after the Trooping of the Colour. We gathered in the Cabinet Room at Number Ten in the early evening, and were regaled with beer and sandwiches. In Wilson's account of his period as Prime Minister from 1974 to 1976 he says that the Government was 'prepared to face a national stoppage if need be, rather than prejudice the pay issue and throughout that weekend it appeared inevitable'. But that is not the way I remember it. He said he wanted to hear our case, so I explained at some length why we would not let railwaymen be treated any differently from other workers in their wage rises. Wilson warned us of the serious economic problems facing the country. Of course, I was well aware that discussions were going on with the TUC at the time to try to reach an understanding on the next pay round. I wondered whether he would really risk a national rail strike at such a delicate stage of the Government's negotations with the TUC.

At the end of our meeting, Wilson stood at the door of the Cabinet Room, having a brief word with each member of my Executive as they left. I was the last to reach him, and he drew me to one side and said we should not do anything drastic and he would see what he could do about getting a settlement.

He was as good as his word. Early the following week Bowman and myself met Tony Crosland, then the Environment Secretary and Michael Foot, who was Employment Secretary, to try and find a solution. Shortly afterwards we returned to the Railways Board expecting to hear of an improved offer. But to my astonishment, the Board's chief negotiator, Bert Farrimond, was as unyielding as ever. I asked him whether anybody had been in touch with him. He said 'No', but then after a short adjournment he came back to the negotiating table in a much more flexible frame of mind and we managed to hammer out a deal that satisfied us. We won rises of 29.8 per cent for railwaymen. The lower paid of our members were helped with a rise in their weekly basic rate from £30.05 a week in two stages to £34.65 a week within two months.

'I am a happy man tonight. All we have done is to establish that Britain's railwaymen are entitled to justice,' I said in an interview. But British Rail Chairman Richard Marsh did not like it at all. He claimed that the settlement would inflict 'enormous damage' on the railway industry, and that 'the dream of an expanded railway has taken a massive setback'. However, my members were well pleased. Not only had the agreement enabled railwaymen to maintain their relative position as compared with the previous year, but the union had also emerged from its midsummer crisis with its reputation enhanced.

The Social Contract 1975-78

The rail crisis over pay in the summer of 1975 helped to strengthen my conviction that we needed an incomes policy in Britain to pull us out of the pay jungle and help to combat inflation. In the face of a catastrophic rise in the rate of inflation to an annual rate of 25 per cent, the leaders of the TUC General Council agreed in July 1975 that there must be voluntary restraint on pay increases during the next negotiating round. The alternative would have been a grave deterioration in the country's economic position, and the possible resignation of the Labour Government.

By a close vote of 19 to 16 the General Council – mainly under the powerful influence of Jack Jones of the Transport and General Workers – agreed that pay rises over the next year were to be only £6 a week for everybody, and nobody with an annual income over £8,500 was to have any increase at all except increments. In my opinion, we had no choice if we were to avoid hyperinflation.

At my first annual conference as General Secretary a few weeks later in St Helier, Jersey, I spoke up strongly in favour of the new £6 policy hammered out by the TUC: 'Can anybody deny that it is necessary to do something to get inflation under control?' I asked. 'You have not got the money in your pocket, but before the ink is dry on the agreement it has evaporated. There may even be a moderate reduction in living standards for some of our people. It would be folly to imagine otherwise. But if the situation is allowed to drift, the unpalatable alternative is staggering unemployment and inflation going through the roof.'

In my view an 'undoubted consequence' of such a catastrophe would be the downfall of the Labour Government and no hope of its return to power for over a decade. The alternative to Labour was a government led by Margaret Thatcher, which, I warned, would bring in 'the most repressive legislation' while at the same time 'exhorting the workers to work harder and more' with a return of massive unemployment. On the other hand, the new Social Contract could be 'a launching pad for the creation of the sort of society' that the NUR had worked for throughout its history. 'Are you going to let it be said that when a Labour government desperately needed help to grapple with the appalling economic problems on a scale never before faced by any previous government, the NUR kicked them in the teeth?' I asked.

While the Conference supported my views with a healthy majority, many of the Executive Committee were far less keen on a pay and prices deal. In May 1976 agreement was reached on a second year of wage restraint, involving a 5 per cent limit on deals with a maximum rise of £4 a week and a minimum one of £2.50 a week. A special Congress of the TUC was held in London on 16 June to endorse this, but I was unable to cast my union's vote for the new deal, because the Executive Committee were deadlocked by 11 votes to 11 over whether to support it, with two members away. Following Scanlon's remark that he had seen into the abyss, the TUC-Labour Government policy was backed by a huge 9.2 million to only 531,000 votes against, but the NUR was compelled to abstain. However, my Executive agreed that we should decide our final attitude at the annual conference in July in Paignton.

The annual conference of the union was always my power base. I found I had far more allies on that body among the seventy-seven delegates than on the Executive Committee, which was already politically divided. Over the years I was able to make sure that the annual conference came to decide all the major issues in the union. The views of the delegates were usually sensible and down to earth, and they were much closer to the thinking of the rank and file at the depots and stations than the Executive Committee.

In 1976 I saw the Social Contract between the Labour Government and the unions developing much further and I spoke enthusiastically for the new pay deal at Paignton. 'The TUC have striven since the earliest days to involve trade unionists in the shaping of government policy on a wide range of issues, particularly those affecting the economy and employment,' I told the delegates.

Having arrived at that position we must be expected to carry a measure of responsibility and we could not simply opt out and leave it to somebody else to solve our problems. I recognized that it was likely to be rough going in the year ahead, but the prize of economic recovery and social advance was worth some sacrifice and some rough justice.

With tragic forethought I told the conference: 'The Tories might give us free collective bargaining but they would also give us three million unemployed.' I was well aware that our members had suffered a real drop in earnings over the previous year because we had agreed to accept cuts in overtime, rest-day and Sunday working to help the Railways Board with their financial troubles, mainly because of the recession and Government action to stem public spending. But I warned delegates that in any free-for-all the railway industry would soon be in a crisis.

The miners' target then was for £100 a week for the coal-face worker, a 49.3 per cent pay rise. Our policy was to ensure that railwaymen and the lowest-rated surface miner should have an equivalent level of earnings. To maintain the cash differential between those two groups would involve a 64.9 per cent pay rise for our members, if the miners reached their objective. This would have added £575 million to the industry's paybills which would rise to £1,475 million, creating an immense pressure on the industry. By 54 votes to 22 the annual conference backed the TUC-Government pay understanding, a convincing majority.

I thought it was absolutely vital that we continued with the Social Contract and did not return to the jungle of free collective bargaining. I was ill and therefore absent from the discussions on the Social Contract in 1977, but the pay guidelines held, and in the winter of 1977-78 the TUC General Council backed pay moderation. I wanted a further understanding on economic policy in 1978 and said so at our Llandudno conference. Although the 1975 pay deal had been welcomed, the benefits we extracted from the Government were soon eaten away by the combined effects of increased taxation, higher National Insurance contributions and a rate of inflation that hit 27 per cent in August 1975. We were actually worse off within a matter of weeks after the settlement than we were when we started. By contrast, in 1977 under phase two of the Social Contract we had achieved a 10 per cent rise for our members when inflation was running at 7 per cent.

In 1977 and 1978 Denis Healey had cut the tax burden so that there was an estimated 6 per cent rise in living standards for workers as a result. My view was: 'I don't care a damn whether members get a rise in their standard of living by pay increases or by a combination of pay increases and tax concessions, because at the end of the day what counts is what you take home in your pay packets to enable the wife to pay the bills.' If there had not been the usual differences between the rail unions over productivity payments at that time our members would have been £2 to £4 a week better off on top of those improvements.

The lesson that the unions should have learned from the crazy free-for-all of 1975 was that you could not look at wages in isolation from the general economic state of the nation, nor for that matter could those who controlled the country's economy afford to ignore wages. 'This is a battle about power, not about 1, 2, 3, 4, 5 or 6 per cent but about who controls Britain for the next twenty years and as to whether we are going to be part of that control,' I told the Llandudno delegates. 'If it makes sense to plan the whole economy when we are in economic distress, surely it must make more sense to plan how we share the newly created wealth that now flows from North Sea oil and the gradually improving economic climate. Do we, as Socialists, believe that the jackpot should be scooped up by those who are prepared to use their industrial muscle? I certainly do not and I think the majority of our members feel the same way. I think all of us should reject this philosophy of the pig trough which advocates that those with the biggest snouts get the biggest share, because that is what it is. This union, with its proud record, ought to reject that philosophy today.'

The mad scramble for higher but ever more worthless wages had nothing whatsoever to do with Socialism: 'If you want more pound notes in your pockets and are not concerned about what they will purchase, all right – ask for 40 per cent. But I am concerned about value for money and raising the standards of our people as a consequence. It makes sense in the public sector to plan how we use our resources in terms of pay. Because of that, but more importantly because I believe in rational Socialist planning, I cannot see how we can plan the economic life of the nation in any other way. That is what public ownership is all about; that is why my grandfather and your grandfathers advocated public ownership, so that we should control the economic life of the nation. Therefore, it is a complete rejection of our beliefs to talk about public ownership and a free-for-all on wages.'

35

But support for an incomes policy did not mean keeping wages static. That would be a total contradiction of all that I have stood for throughout my life. My job was to fight to raise the standards of the people I represented. The question was simply how best to campaign and work for these improvements and for the elimination of hardship and injustice.

I believe in collective bargaining and I have always done so, but I argued in 1978 that it was the kind, the method and the application of that bargaining which was at stake: 'I want to see collective bargaining through the mobilization of the strength of 11½ million members of unions affiliated to the TUC acting through the TUC bargaining with the Government of the day. In my view we should be prepared to sit down with the Labour Government to discuss a joint plan for the next twelve months. Those discussions should cover a whole range of economic decisions, not only affecting pay, but investment, social services, unemployment, in fact the whole social and economic fabric of national policy.'

A prices and incomes policy should 'benefit workers, maintain an orderly control of the allocation of resources to labour costs and keep industrial relations at a level which resembled rational behaviour by reasonable people, rather than the savage, cat-and-dog fights which were the traditional methods of settling problems of pay and conditions of working'.

'Whether we shall take the rational way forward depends upon the willingness of the movement to sit down seriously and discuss urgently with this Government a further Social Contract. Let us range over the whole of the field of things that affect the lives of the British people and all our members, including education, housing and standards of living in every way and every sense. Let us strike a fair bargain with them.'

What I wanted was a 'bargain' that would raise living standards for trade unionists and keep us going in the right direction. We shared economic difficulties and burdens with the Labour Government between 1975 and 1977, so I simply could not understand why when things were getting much better we could not sit down together and co-operate on how to distribute the wealth that would be coming from North Sea oil. My speech won the approval of a majority of the delegates, and by a margin of 50 votes to 27 the NUR continued to back the Social Contract. I was helped in my cause with a powerful speech made on the same day at the conference by the then Prime Minister, Jim Callaghan.

I have a high regard for Callaghan. He is the first politician to have held each of the four major offices of state – the Treasury, Home Office, Foreign Office and the Premiership. His trade union background gave him a feel for the Labour Party and he conveyed to the British people the image of Labour they understood: the party of fairness, the party that ordinary people could instinctively turn to for hope and guidance. His record in office from 1976 to 1979 has been criticized unjustly. Under his government public ownership and the National Health Service were expanded. More doctors and nurses were recruited. More students went to university. And at the end of his period as Prime Minister old age pensioners were 20 per cent better off in real terms. He delivered 95 per cent of the October 1974 Labour manifesto.

Callaghan wanted to establish a further understanding with the TUC. The whole TUC General Council was invited to see him and his senior ministers at Number Ten on 18 July 1978, during Llandudno. It turned out to be an historic occasion. The Prime Minister started by expressing the hope that at least a closer understanding would emerge of the positions and responsibilities of the TUC as well as the Government. Denis Healey, the Chancellor of the Exchequer, followed him saying that the Government could not avoid taking a view about pay rises for the 13 million people working in the public sector and that it would be neither practicable nor desirable to have guidelines for the public sector and none for the private sector. The Government wanted to give the maximum of flexibility compatible with the general pay guidelines and this might involve 'kitty' bargaining and productivity deals, with cuts in hours only as long as they did not increase costs.

But Len Murray, speaking for the majority of the TUC General Council, replied that there was a danger that the Government was becoming unduly preoccupied with wages and creating an impression that was not helpful to foreign confidence. He suggested that Ministers appeared to underrate the difficulties the present pay policy was causing, which would multiply the longer the pay restraint continued. He stressed the need for union negotiators to be able to deal with particular situations and their ability to make positive contributions to investment and productivity. Murray thought that the Government overlooked the fact that union negotiators would have a general wish not to go back to the inflationary conditions of 1974-75, and that ministers might help

37

to improve the climate for bargaining by action on prices, employment and expansion and an increase in public spending.

Callaghan responded that the Government must remain preoccupied with pay for the simple reason that expectations in the past had been too high and they would have to be reduced to more reasonable levels before the Government could cease to be preoccupied. The Prime Minister admitted to us that there would be no attempt to introduce pay legislation: his only weapon would be persuasion and public opinion. The aim of the meeting, he said, was to try and persuade the unions to accept a moderate round of wage increases after August 1978. He said he took the view that it would be desirable every year to have discussions with the TUC and the employers on what level of wage rises was appropriate for the economy. He did not wish to place all the burdens of the economy on the trade union movement, but he felt that he would have to give clear guidance on methods of achieving single-figure inflation as the basis for the future growth in living standards. He argued that wage rises in the coming pay round would have to be well below the level they had reached in the present round if single-figure inflation was to be maintained in 1979.

That sombre meeting in Downing Street sealed the fate of the Labour Government. It had provided the opportunity to establish a renewed Social Contract, bringing the TUC into a more decisive role in the running of the economy. I have spent my whole career at negotiating tables and I can certainly say that if ever we were presented with an opportunity to negotiate, it was then. But the TUC General Council simply did not want to know. Most of the union leaders only felt at home in the harsh world of free collective bargaining that they knew. As the discussion went on, the hopes of a new bargain between the unions and the Government vanished before my eyes. It was a bitter moment. I began to be deeply anxious about what would happen in the coming winter: there was a real prospect of a senseless pay explosion.

Without our agreement, the Government announced a 5 per cent target for increases in the next pay round starting in August 1978. The TUC General Council rejected it.

The Winter of Discontent 1978-79
What was especially depressing to me was that those union leaders who argued for an incomes policy and a further Social Contract with Labour won the backing of their union conferences that

summer. Indeed, the late Glyn Phillips, President of the National and Local Government Officers' Association (NALGO), moved a resolution at September's Trades Union Congress which, although it condemned any unilateral policies of wage restraint, also pointed out that free collective bargaining had never been a reality in the public services. NALGO, a union which was not even affiliated to the Labour Party, proposed a 'new approach to pay' which would be within 'the framework of an economic contract with the Government' of a long-term character. This would have involved flexible wage guidelines through talks with employers, unions and Government, as well as reflationary measures through increased public spending to boost demand for goods and services; price and dividend restrictions; protection for the low paid; and improvements in child benefits and pensions.

I seconded the NALGO motion, using many of the arguments that I had made in my Llandudno speech to my union conference. I hoped that after Congress we could all sit down together and work out a common economic strategy, because I believed we would be driven to speak the language of Socialism and we would be able to agree on priorities.

But the NALGO motion found few other backers in the trade union movement. Only Tom Jackson from the Post Office Workers threw his eloquent support behind the proposal. I am utterly convinced that if other union leaders had also argued the case for an incomes policy with their own members they would have won the necessary support to make a deal, but they didn't even try. They took the view that we had sustained the policy far too long, and that strong pressure from the extreme Left was making it difficult for them. Despite the rejection of the NALGO-NUR approach on a new deal with the Government on economic policy, Congress was on its best behaviour that week because we all thought that Jim Callaghan was going to call a general election at any moment and union leaders did not want to incur any blame for hurting Labour's chances. But then, on the Thursday night in the week of Congress, he suddenly went on television and announced that he was not going to the country that autumn but intended to soldier on into 1979.

To be fair to Callaghan, his advisors had warned against an election that autumn, but it was a bad error. Many union leaders felt a sense of betrayal. I was personally dismayed at Callaghan's decision and worried that he would find it hard to hold any line on pay deals through the winter, though even I didn't realize just how ferocious the wages scramble was going to be, and I am sure that Callaghan in his wildest dreams never anticipated what would happen.

We soon had a foretaste of coming events, when the Labour Party conference met a few weeks later in Blackpool in early October. A resolution was moved by the hard Left-dominated Liverpool Wavertree constituency party that rejected 'totally any wage restraint by whatever method, including cash limits and specifically the Government's 5 per cent'. It suggested wage curbs were not welcomed 'by the working class' and would 'lead to a possible rejection of the Labour Party by the people who fought for the return of a Labour Government in 1974'.

The motion went on to demand immediate Government withdrawal from intervention in wage negotiations, and recognition of the right of trade unions to negotiate freely on behalf of their members. The planning of wages would apparently have to wait for the creation of a socialist economy, after we had reached the Promised Land.

Union leaders queued up at the rostrum to bury the Social Contract. Alan Fisher of the National Union of Public Employees (NUPE) demanded that nobody should have a wage less than two-thirds of national average earnings and his members would be fighting to achieve a £60 a week basic minimum, a 40 per cent rise. Joe Gormley of the Mineworkers told delegates that it was 'time the trade union movement was allowed to do its job in a responsible and sensible way, without interference by anybody'. He said to Callaghan: 'For God's sake, trust us.' Gavin Laird of the Amalgamated Union of Engineering Workers (AUEW) argued that the Cabinet did not have 'the sole prerogative of intelligence in economic thinking .... We have accepted Social Contracts and, comrade Callaghan, we are not prepared to accept any more and certainly not a 5 per cent norm.'

In that highly emotional atmosphere in Blackpool's Winter Gardens, I managed to get to the rostrum. There is no point at all in mincing your words when you speak in the Labour movement. You only get five or six minutes to say your piece, so you must get to the guts of the issue pretty quickly if you want to make an impact. You need to be blunt and to the point, especially on issues of such major importance. A 'softly, softly' approach is no good at all. I recall my grandfather telling me: 'If you can't say what you want to say in ten minutes you must be telling lies.' You need to be especially forceful in the heat of the cauldron of the Labour Party conference, amid the howling from those who don't want to listen to the truth. My speech at the 1978 party conference certainly raised the temperature but I was angry at hearing nonsense about the wages free-for-all when so much was at stake, and as I walked to the rostrum I decided to make this plain.

I won some applause to start with when I reminded delegates of Nye Bevan's belief that Socialism was 'the language of priorities', and so whether we liked it or not the whole movement would have to decide those priorities when they talked about Britain's economic strategy. I then denounced the Wavertree motion as an 'emotional spasm, based on nothing', and went on to spell out the real consequences that would attend a free-for-all on pay: 'If Alan Fisher wants to get out from under the bottom of the pile – Alan, you have got to support motion 38 [backing the Social Contract] because if you do not I will tell you what is going to happen. You say, "Let's get 40 per cent." That is what you want. Forty per cent in my industry will mean £320 million on the pay bill. You tell me fares will not go up. Let me tell you this. If you get 40 per cent, Alan, in your world, I am going to get 40. And the difference between you and me: I have got some power to do it with. And to Joe Gormley – Joe, if your members get 40 per cent, we are getting it, because you can produce as much coal as you like, you will not get it moved.'

I was ready to accept within a Socialist economic strategy that we would 'run a little slower in order that Alan and NUPE can run a bit quicker' and even to forego differential rises for some of our higher-paid members if we could get a socialist incomes policy. 'I do not like the 5 per cent any more than you do. But the 5 per cent is there because the trade union movement abdicated its responsibilities.... Because I was in Downing Street on 18 July when the Prime Minister said: "Can we reason this out together?" And he was told by Len Murray, speaking for the TUC, "Leave it to us – and trust us. We will bargain responsibly." There are 112 unions with General Secretaries and Executive Committees. If they were left to determine the pay policy, they would not know what the hell to do.'

Some delegates laughed at that remark, but I pointed to the big wage demands that were being lined up that autumn, such as the 20 per cent pay rise and 35-hour working week claim at Ford. 'That is what they call responsible collective bargaining. Responsible.

Really? When I entered this movement – and I am the third generation in it – my union helped to create this party, the union that sponsored the conference that created the Labour Party. I am not going to stand here and destroy it. But if you want the call to go out at this conference that the new philosophy in the Labour party you believe in is the philosophy of the pig trough – those with the biggest snout get the biggest share – I reject it. My union rejects it. And if I am the only one standing here saying it, I will reject it until I drop down dead.'

I was aware that many union leaders didn't like the 'pig trough' reference which I had first made at my own conference in the summer, but it was the truth and they knew it. You have to use forceful imagery like that to drive home the issue to people. Of course, it was not what the 1978 Labour party conference wanted to hear, especially the extremists, and, despite a brave speech from Michael Foot urging caution, delegates voted to back the Wavertree motion by a massive 4,017,000 votes to only 1,924,000 against.

Even after that defeat I continued to press the case in the TUC for a prices and incomes policy, but efforts to avoid a wages explosion failed. The General Council tied 17 votes to 17 on a form of words we had cobbled together for responsible collective bargaining. I was under the impression that we were not going to vote on this and had left the meeting earlier. But even if I had been present when a vote was forced, and had ensured a majority for the motion, it would not have mattered as the wording was pretty wishy-washy and involved no real commitment.

Two days after Christmas I warned in an article in the *Guardian* that there was 'a very real danger of social breakdown worse than that which led to the rise of Fascism and Nazism'. And I went on: 'Those who now clamour for a free-for-all in pay are subscribing to the wholly discredited and disgraceful theory that "might is right".' I also drew attention to the Tory attitude. 'Mrs Thatcher thinks by splitting hairs – free-for-all No; freedom under the law for all Yes – she can deceive the people. The people who run the Tory Party never change. They want freedom to exploit, to gain, to win in an unequal fight.' It was not just the hard Left but also the Tories who were cheering on the Ford car workers and the demands for free collective bargaining. But I was fully conscious of the dangers that arose from the extreme Left, of how they would welcome the approaching chaos as a chance to create their 'new society' out of 'the breakdown of the present system'. 'If that was the way to get it I would subscribe to the supposition,' I wrote. 'But history says otherwise. I believe that given rational behaviour on all sides we can avoid the brutal offence of harmful war. That has been our plea from the start.

'Recognizing that there are, in fact, conflicting aims and sources of dispute about the making and distribution of wealth, we want the trade union movement as the most significant controller of economic power through labour organization to participate in the making of planning decisions covering the whole range of economic and social issues. It is the only way for civilized people to work. The alternative is a series of steps descending to confrontation and repression and open warfare. The first steps have already been taken – rejection of the Social Contract and the drift of the trade union movement into a conglomerate of savage, vested interests fighting to get the biggest bone....'

My grim prophecies of industrial conflict were confirmed by the turbulent events of early 1979, when one group of public service workers after another struck for massive wage rises, bringing misery to thousands of people. Schools were closed. Hospitals were put under siege. Dustbins were left unemptied. The dead were left unburied on Merseyside. The so-called 'Winter of Discontent' did terrible moral damage to the trade union movement. It paved the way for the victory of Margaret Thatcher in May 1979. It seemed to me a sheer betrayal of the values of trade unionism, a selfish and self-destructive struggle that mocked our Socialist faith. On the TUC General Council we drifted along, apparently powerless to do anything about the mayhem in the country. Eventually a 'Concordat' was signed between the TUC and the Labour Government, setting out joint economic and social priorities for the future and a code of industrial conduct for unions to follow.

But all of this was far too late and the damage had been done. I have no doubt that Callaghan had been wrong to pitch the pay target figure as low as 5 per cent, but I saw this as primarily his first bargaining position. If the TUC had been ready to negotiate with him, that figure would have been improved. The unions must take the full blame for Labour's electoral disaster in May 1979. I said that at the 1982 TUC, and delegates howled at me for saying so, but they knew I was right. I had touched some raw nerves.

The National Economic Assessment
After the May 1979 defeat I became more convinced than ever that

any future Labour Government needed to achieve a firm agreement with the TUC on all economic issues before it came to office. For much of the next four years I became something of a lone voice among trade union leaders in talking this way, particularly when I advocated the planning of wages.

I have never really understood how people who claim to be good Socialists can also be such fervent believers in the wages jungle. I used to go on an annual pilgrimage to the Scottish TUC to give the Communists there some basic lessons in the fundamentals of Socialism. The Mineworkers' Vice-President Mick McGahey was my prime target on those occasions. The delegates used to cat-call at first, but over the years they came to listen to me with more respect. I did not convince many of them about the error of their ways, but at least I made some think harder about the wages issue, which I regard as absolutely vital to the work of the unions in a managed economy. Apparently some of the hard Left said they missed me when I was not at the 1983 Scottish TUC, so I must have made some impression on them.

Many union leaders must have got fed up with me for going on about the need for a planned incomes strategy as part of a wider deal between the unions and the Labour Party, but I saw no good reason why I should shut up about it just because the party was now in opposition. In fact, the philosophy of Mrs Thatcher as it came into practice made me even surer that what I was saying was crucial for our future. It is a pity other union leaders did not see this as well.

Mrs Thatcher's Government has sought to squeeze the trade unions out of any role at all in the economic management of the country. Our involvement in politics is blamed by her for wrecking Britain's prosperity. But I reject totally the Conservative view which would relegate the unions to the sidelines. They are not going to be bashed into oblivion by the slump and anti-trade union legislation. There is little doubt about the power of the trade unions in this country: if you include the families of trade unionists, more than half the population of this country is linked to the trade union movement. The question that has always concerned me is: how can that power be put to constructive use?

All the successful economies of western Europe – such as West Germany, Austria and the Scandinavian countries – believe in and practice an industrial consensus between what they call the 'social partners' of industry and labour. A partnership of that kind is impossible with Mrs Thatcher, but I am sure that it remains the only real hope for Britain if we are to become a more prosperous and dynamic country.

I have never supported a policy on incomes that involved the Government in practising compulsion on unwilling workers. The right way to do it has always been by getting consent, hammering out an agreement that all sides can honour. Wage freezes imposed by the Government, or statutory restraint around a certain wage norm for everybody backed up by penal sanctions, cannot last for long. After a short time they fall apart, leaving the disease they set out to cure more virulent than ever. The real need is for parameters within which the trade unions would be able to carry out their traditional function as collective bargainers.

But how were we to go about reaching agreement on the level of wage rises which the economy could sustain in a given period? The plain fact is that you cannot reconcile trade union insistence on planning the resources of the nation in the interests of the people, if on the other hand you leave incomes to be settled in the market place. It is sheer nonsense to talk about planning and to leave out of account the 70 per cent of national income made up of wages and salaries. There is no point in ducking the issue.

We have to find a solution to this problem, which has caused repeated difficulties inside the Labour movement since 1945. Time and again Labour governments have sown the seeds of their election defeat by their failure to reach agreement with the unions on the crucial wages question: in the late forties under Clement Attlee, in the sixties under Harold Wilson and again in the seventies under Jim Callaghan.

The beginnings of a new approach to this problem appeared in some of the words in the ill-fated 'Concordat' signed by the TUC and the Labour Government in February 1979. It suggested that each year, before Easter, there should be 'a national assessment by Government and both sides of industry of our economic prospects which would take all factors and the relations between them into account'. Jim Callaghan, too, spoke of this approach, in his May 1979 general election manifesto, in terms which fitted in with my own thinking.

Through the TUC-Labour Party Liaison Committee we moved slowly towards a firmer understanding on those lines. The method proposed by this body is known as the National Economic Assessment, and it was supported in principle by both the TUC and the

Labour Party conference in 1981, although the TUC in 1982 also voted to reject talks with any Government on pay restraint. Up to that time I had not had much joy in getting articles in the Communist *Morning Star* and I complained about it and as a result they relented and let me in on my support for incomes policy. I wrote the article immediately after the 1982 Congress, attacking the Communist attitude to pay bargaining. I could understand the Communist Party's anxiety about the mounting support among the unions for the National Economic Assessment, because it proposed a stable framework for the expansion of real incomes within the context of a planned Socialist approach to the economy.

'Nothing could be further removed from that state of industrial warfare upon which the Communist Party now depends as its sole source of influence inside the Labour movement,' I wrote. In my opinion the policies agreed at the TUC in September 1982 amounted to a 'major advance in the direction of social justice and Socialist planning', and they 'clearly established the central role of the trade union movement in the economic management of the nation.' The National Economic Assessment is not a policy to impose norms or fixed limits on pay; indeed it was designed to avoid the previous experience of elevating policy on wages to the over-riding consideration of economic strategy. There is no question of regulating collective bargaining in the workplace by means of the Assessment. But on the other hand, it does recognize what is only common sense: that the pay of workers (including the 14 million who are paid by the State by way of benefits) forms an essential part of the annual discussions. The TUC envisages the Assessment as an extension of collective bargaining, tackling the question of priorities between investment, taxation, the social wage, considering how much money can be made available for improving and adjusting incomes. The policy has been gaining support from unions, although there is opposition from groups like the Communist Party.

The TUC still manages to face both ways on the pay issue, and this has to be changed. As I have said, 'The trade unions cannot afford the luxury of "wait and see" before we take on our responsibilities under the next Labour Government. If we are to make real progress towards a Socialist society, we must begin to build it from Labour's first day in power.'

Over the winter of 1982-83 the TUC-Labour Party liaison committee worked to put some substance into the National Economic Assessment, and in March 1983 the two participants announced a joint economic programme for the next Labour Government, which spelt out clearly what the new approach would involve. It was very much on the lines of what I had been fighting for during all my years as NUR General Secretary.

Progress to a better understanding on economic issues has been painfully slow inside the TUC, and we may yet still find the consensus of support for the National Economic Assessment does not outlast the problems of the next few years, but at least many union leaders now realize that the pay free-for-all is not a sensible way to help their members or the country to achieve a real economic advance.

Labour and the Rail Crisis 1975-79

Running the railways

For most of my eight eventful years as the NUR's General Secretary the railway industry suffered badly either from the threat of heavy cutbacks or from deliberate financial neglect by Governments of both major political parties. Indeed, ever since the nationalization of the network in 1947 the railways have struggled to find their proper role in the economic and industrial life of the country, and no Government since 1951 has had a clearly defined overall transport policy.

I am a strong believer in public ownership. I always have been. My union favoured nationalization as long ago as 1894, not only because its leaders and members believed it was in the best interests for railway workers, bringing them improved pay and conditions, but also because the whole community would benefit as well.

But sadly, Governments have constantly interfered in the running of the railways, often in a negative and even a hostile way. We have lurched from one short-term expedient to another. Over the years since 1947 no fewer than eighteen Ministers have been responsible for transport policy. I had to deal with seven of them in eight years. There have been as many as nine major pieces of legislation on transport, with many more concerned indirectly with the railways. We have suffered from a complete lack of stability. While most European countries have demonstrated a much more positive attitude to railways regardless of the political colour of individual governments, here the railways have faced a

48

constant uphill struggle to win support from Ministers and their civil servants.

The road lobby has proved to be much more powerful than ourselves in influencing Government policy. Organizations like the Road Haulage Association (RHA) and unions such as the TGWU have usually adopted a fervently pro-road policy, and their voices have carried much greater weight in Whitehall than those of the railway interest. Far more civil servants, for example, are employed by the Department of Transport to deal with roads than there are for the railways.

Being Chairman of the Railways Board has become a near-impossible job in recent times, with a constant struggle for limited resources in the face of unsympathetic Governments. Political intervention has been never-ending. I remember one Chairman, Sir Stanley Raymond, at a negotiating session with us when I was Assistant General Secretary. He was suddenly called away to speak to the Minister, Barbara Castle, on the phone. He came back and carried on with the discussion without turning a hair, but later we learned that the phone call had been to tell him that he had been fired.

Sir Richard Marsh, the former Labour Minister of Transport, was Board Chairman when I became General Secretary in 1975. He was not there long enough during my time for me to reach any close understanding with him. In my view I am not really sure he was cut out to manage an industry the size and importance of British Rail. There is a world of a difference between being a politician and the chairman of a nationalized enterprise. To run one of our public services industrial experience is needed as one must be given the freedom to manage, without having to look over the shoulder all the time to find out what the Minister thinks. I don't recall ever visiting Marsh in his office and having a man-to-man talk with him on any issue. I only met him at formal set-piece occasions, although I did invite him to our annual conference in 1975.

Sir Peter Parker was totally different. He was also a Labour Party member, but he had experience in industry and a highly successful record there. He was offered British Rail in 1967 and turned it down, but in 1970 he became Chairman-designate of what was to be the nationalized Ports Authority, ready to start work if Labour had won the general election. In the event he returned to private industry until he was appointed to the Railways Board in 1975. He at once got in touch with me and we had a good working relationship from Day One.

Parker was the eternal optimist, full of hope and energy, eager to learn. In later years I used to say to him: 'For God's sake, Peter. Don't smile at me when we are examining the Board's problems. From where I am sitting they look awful.' I also told him: 'I think you smile because you are too old to cry.'

He went out of his way to keep close to the unions, and I think this helped him later on in his delicate dealings with the Government. I wanted to work with him to make a success of British Rail. I believe the best way of proving the case for public ownership is to set the example of an efficient industry serving the nation's needs and providing the sort of good pay and conditions that a productive labour force deserves. I invited Parker to come and speak to our annual conferences, allowing him as much time as he needed to address the delegates. He was subjected to questions, and would listen to our debates. I felt this was vital to mutual understanding.

Even though Parker had no background in the railways, he had first-hand experience of the problems of managing a big business. It did not take him long to work his way into the job and he became a first-class advocate of the railways. He knew how to handle the media and he used them in an aggressive way to champion rail travel. He generated a sincere concern for the future of the industry. On his initiative we created the Rail Council, at which the Presidents and General Secretaries of all the railway unions and the Chairman and senior members of the Board met frequently to discuss the industry's problems.

Established in the autumn of 1979, the Rail Council was very much his idea. It is a unique body, bringing together the Railways Board and the three rail unions to discuss a wide range of policy issues on the future of the industry. The Chairman even told us what he had in mind before all of his Board were informed.

An effort was made to establish a genuine partnership between us in support of the railway system. It was a very good idea, giving the rail unions a direct and influential say in the making of policy before any final decisions were taken. This is the kind of open, democratic involvement that remains possible in a nationalized enterprise, but is rarely seen in private industry. Unfortunately the rail crises after 1980 did much to undermine the mutual confidence that was vital to the success of the Rail Council. I know perfectly well that Parker and I had slightly different priorities, but the ultimate objective of an efficient, highly popular industry carrying masses of freight and people and serving the nation was common to us both. I often used to think what a team we would have made, if he and I had been able to work together with only one union in the industry.

In my view, what prevented Parker from making the great advances he had in mind for the industry was that he underestimated the sheer size of the railways and their problems. You cannot make an immediate impact in that job. You have constantly to be on top of your renewal programme – the track, signalling, rolling stock. If you allow it to run on, you build up a backlog you cannot overcome without massive investment. The recession made it worse for him. It dealt severe blows to the freight business and receipts fell, but you can't close down the network to compensate for the losses. Nor can you put the whole system on to short time or a four-day week if demand slackens. The entire network must be kept going twenty-four hours a day seven days a week whatever happens. Parker also had to face an intolerable trade union situation, unparalleled in any other industry, which created enormous problems for him.

He has left British Rail a disappointed man because he knew what the industry required but the forces ranged against him made his task impossible. It will be a long time before the Government can persuade anybody of his ability to take on the task of running the railway network. There is a lesson here for the unions who claim to believe in public ownership: we need to make a much greater effort to make the nationalized industries work than we do.

The crisis over Crosland

I had hoped that after Labour returned to power in February 1974 we would have a coherent transport policy. But soon after our pay crisis in July 1975 I realized that the Government was getting ready to do an about-face in its support for public transport and the railways in particular. The October 1974 general election manifesto had actually pledged Labour to move as much traffic as possible from road to rail and to water and to develop public transport to make us less dependent on the private car. The Labour Party might have lacked any detailed transport strategy but at least the overall general principles were clear enough, or so I thought.

However, in the autumn of 1975 the Board made it clear to us that the Government was insisting that the railway industry should accept cuts in its spending programmes. During the previous four years the unions and Transport 2000 had been pressing for a co-ordinated transport system and a much higher priority for public transport. But now the rumours coming out of Whitehall suggested the anti-rail lobby was gaining the upper hand again.

I feared we might even be on the brink of another era of rail cuts on the massive scale of those imposed by Beeching twelve years earlier. We assembled a delegation to see John Gilbert, the junior Minister at the Department of the Environment responsible for transport, but he did nothing to calm our worries about the Government's intentions.

The Board told us privately that the financial restrictions being placed on the industry's investment plans would have a grave impact on the future of the network. The fact that Labour was in office was apparently making little difference to attitudes. Contrary to what we had reasonably expected, the unions had no instant access to senior Ministers to set forth their case. In fact, it was quite the reverse. I did not meet Tony Crosland during all the time he was in charge of the Department of the Environment. It was not until later, when I was on a trip to China over 7,000 miles away that I bumped into him at the British Embassy in Peking – by that time he was Foreign Secretary.

Apparently, Crosland found transport uninteresting at first. Then suddenly he took a keen interest in the subject, but he got it into his head that rail travel was just a pastime for the rich who could well afford to pay high fares. He saw no good reason why the taxpayer should be asked to foot the bill to help the well-off commuters in South-East England and Inter-City businessmen to get to and from their offices. But I always thought this was a nonsensical argument. It was only true to the extent that the lowest income groups travel very little indeed by any means, for obvious reasons. If subsidies for the railways were not justified because more affluent people used trains, then I wondered what the justification could be for Government support for the car industry or inland air services, let alone Concorde. Furthermore, rail for leisure travel attracts people from all income groups.

The threat to the commuters was real enough. But again I thought it was wrongly conceived. Many young couples looking to buy their own home have been forced to move away from city centres and further from their jobs, and they would face real hardship if they were to be forced to pay massive fares.

I used to travel to work by train from my home at Bishop's Stortford and I saw no real evidence to back up Crosland's prejudices. My fellow passengers looked ordinary people to me and not so well off. A crazy escalation in fares would certainly have made Crosland's argument come true, but then simply because only the very rich would be able to travel by train.

Our worries were not just imaginary. Rail fares went up by more than 50 per cent in 1975. There were also cuts in weekend and holiday services, a virtual stop to all recruiting of staff and a holding back of some investment projects. The Government announced that rail passenger grants for 1976 were to be kept (in real terms) within the 1975 figure, despite the rise in inflation. Ceilings were to be set to keep the total level of support and borrowing down, while the freight losses were to be eliminated as soon as possible.

In November 1975 I decided we could wait no longer for the Government's promised Consultative Document on transport before mounting a counter-attack against the anti-rail threats. A 'No Rail Cuts' campaign was launched to alert public opinion.

I got into a public slanging match with Crosland over what was happening. He suggested in the House of Commons that stories in the press about massive cuts on the railways were 'a load of old codswallop', but I retorted bitterly that he was a 'bloody liar' for saying so. The Board had kept us fully informed on Government pressures and we knew the industry could not stand the kind of financial austerity demanded without widespread cuts in services. I was convinced that Crosland was on the point of betraying every policy that the Labour Party had adopted in the transport field since the turn of the century, and it seemed to me that it was about time the Government came clean about their intentions.

In April 1976 Crosland published his Consultation Document. It confirmed our worst fears. The report was one of the most blatantly biased Government presentations I had ever laid eyes on. If it had been produced by one of the road lobby pressure groups I would have recognized the prejudice and accepted it as such, but this document was supposed to represent the balanced view of the Government. Yet how could genuine consultation with the public take place if the facts were so twisted and distorted to suit the inbuilt prejudices of the author?

53

Ironically, the Labour Government seemed to be undoing the progress made when John Peyton was Transport Minister under the Tories in 1973. The Heath government had appeared to be backing the introduction of the High Speed diesels and development of the Advanced Passenger Train for Inter-City. Commuter services were to be improved with new rolling stock and electrification, while there was to be massive investment in new signalling and track. Of course, that is not the same as saying that the Tories would have carried out these plans if they had stayed in power.

The proposals in the Crosland document were designed to cut the railways to pieces. It suggested that further fare rises would not reduce the volume of passenger traffic. Apparently, 'higher subsidies could be paid only at the expense of other vital programmes and would not be socially justified.' On Inter-City services, the Government was suggesting that the aim should be to cover all their allocated costs by 1981. Commuters in the outer suburbs of London were given five years to prepare for meeting the full cost of their travel. This was apparently 'long enough to enable people to make any adjustments in their way of life with the minimum of inconvenience'. For loss-making rural services it was suggested a subsidized bus service would provide a sensible substitute.

The document suggested that 'difficult choices' had to be made on future investment. It gave a number of options, including a concentration on essential renewals of track and signalling; a more selective approach to product improvement; limiting further electrification; a 'less comfortable and slower service' and a 'slower introduction' of the High Speed and Advanced Passenger Trains.

Crosland's paper also dismissed as a 'pipe-dream' the suggestion that a large amount of long-distance freight traffic could be shifted from the roads to rail. I did not accept this sweeping conclusion. It should be possible under conditions of fair competition for British Rail to carry long-distance bulk traffic, but the massive subsidies going to the lorry operators to the tune of £1,700 a year per lorry was simply not mentioned in the document, nor the cost of the motorway programme to the taxpayer.

The Consultative Document concluded that if the current British Rail deficit was to be kept at even its present record levels, there would have to be 'drastic economies, or substantial fare rises, or cuts in services'. And it added: 'The most likely recipe is a mixture in some proportion of all these ingredients. To the extent that any one remedy is forsworn, the burden will have to be that much greater on the others.' The whole tone and content of that paper were surprisingly similar to the findings of the Serpell inquiry on railway finance published in January 1983.

I realized that we would have to launch a massive campaign of opposition to the Government's consultative paper, both inside and outside Parliament, if the railway network was to be saved from the axe. All three rail unions and the Board had to work together to convince outside opinion that its implementation would mean a death sentence for the existing system.

In a way, Crosland's anti-rail document came to us as a blessing in disguise, though a rather heavily disguised blessing when you read its contents. It forced us to concentrate our energies on producing a response which would be a positive contribution to the transport debate and not a negative defence of the status quo. As a result the NUR published its *Policy for Transport* in July 1976, which prepared the way for a giant step towards our long-term goal of a planned transport policy.

I saw the conflict as being not between road and rail but between public and private transport. The motor car had to be restrained, particularly in the cities and towns, but it was nonsense to advocate this unless it was coupled with greater provision of both bus and rail public transport. On the freight side, the railways should undertake the long hauls not just for bulk goods but general merchandise as well, preferably between rail sidings at the customer's premises, while other local delivery could be left to lorries. If the Labour Government had accepted our proposals we should have been well on the way to providing a transport policy which would meet the needs of the people and make a valuable contribution to the country's economic recovery.

I made it quite clear to the Government that my union would fight to preserve and improve the existing railway system. We aroused some criticism when we suggested that the NUR-sponsored Labour MPs should withdraw their support from the Government if it refused to drop its anti-rail policies. But feelings were running high and I was absolutely determined to make sure that Ministers took serious notice of what we were saying and changed their minds. There was no good reason why my union should go on pouring money into the Labour Party and giving faithful support to the Government, if they refused to listen to us.

Large-scale lobbying took place through 1976 and into 1977 to convince Ministers not to swallow the Consultative Document.

Private lunches and dinners were organized with senior Cabinet Ministers, including Michael Foot and Anthony Wedgwood Benn, to win their backing. We mobilized the Labour Party as well as the TUC against the Crosland strategy. An immense amount of time and effort was devoted to the 'No Rail Cuts' campaign.

Peter Shore became Environment Secretary soon after the paper was published, but although he assured my annual conference in July 1976 that 'no major butchery' of the rail network was threatened, he failed to allay our fears. Not until Bill Rodgers was made Transport Minister did we find a man who was prepared at least to listen to what we had to say. Indeed, of the seven transport ministers I had to deal with in eight years, he was the most sympathetic to the rail cause.

In the winter of 1976-77 we tried to make Rodgers realize that an investment ceiling of £217.5 million a year on public expenditure on the railways would inevitably mean a rundown of the system, because it would not be possible to carry through the necessary track renewal, speed restrictions would have to be introduced on many lines, the antiquated signalling equipment would remain, and a phased-down plan for the new High Speed Trains would add to British Rail's problems.

The Government's White Paper on transport was long delayed, but rumours early in 1977 continued to suggest Ministers were still ready to take a tough attitude to freight and the Inter-City services, arguing that both should somehow pay their way. The considered response to the debate on the Crosland document was eventually published in June 1977 and it came as something of a relief. The Government appeared to have accepted many of our arguments, and Ministers were less enthusiastic about road transport. There was a more positive tone to the White Paper. Instead of going on about the rising cost of revenue support for the industry as Crosland had done, the document actually accepted that a 'substantial and continuing commitment' was needed to maintain public transport because the income raised from fares was simply not enough to ensure a reasonable level of services being available.

The problems of rural transport services were to be resolved through more flexibility in the vehicle licensing laws so that bus and mini-bus companies could meet local needs. We were reassured by the Government's commitment to a five-year rolling programme of investment for the railways in locomotives and air-braked wagons.

The White Paper made it clear that any idea of massive cutbacks in the railway system had been ruled out. But the document was still unsatisfactory in some ways. It said nothing about the need for an accelerated electrification programme and it postponed a decision on the future of Freightliners and National Carriers, which we wanted to see back under British Rail. Opportunities for a bolder approach were missed.

The Transport Act 1978 went a good deal further. It returned Freightliners Ltd to British Rail, something for which we had been campaigning since 1969 when it had been hived off. Moreover, the National Freight Corporation, under the new legislation, was put under an obligation to ensure that freight went by rail whenever such a way of moving goods was 'efficient and economic'.

I don't think we really won much of a victory. We did put a stop to some of the more drastic threats to the railways posed by Crosland which would certainly have been implemented if the Consultative Document had been turned into Government policy. But all our energies for over three years had been spent on trying to head off the dangers to the industry. We did not manage to take the offensive in a constructive way with the Labour Government to win ministerial approval for positive plans for the railways. Instead we marked time for that period, while the railway network continued to fray around its edges.

One thing we had pressed hard for was a firm Government commitment on rail electrification as soon as possible, and the union drew up its own proposals. The cost savings on fuel by moving to electrification were considerable, but Britain was lagging far behind the rest of Europe in electrifying track. Now the Government appeared to take a more positive attitude towards electrification, and Rodgers set up a fresh joint review in July 1978 to look at the general case for electrifying all the main lines.

Export orders to British Rail engineering workshops were also becoming buoyant. In 1978 the income derived for British Rail from sales overseas was ten times more than two years previously. Rodgers even expressed the personal view that the building of a Channel rail tunnel would go ahead in the future.

Unfortunately, far too many crucial decisions on the future of the railways had still not been made when Labour left office. Indeed, it is only during the past few years in Opposition that the Labour Party has managed to hammer out a coherent transport policy which provides a key role for the railways. For the first time, all the unions in the transport industries came together and reached agreement on what needed to be done. Several conferences were held at the NUR's training college of Frant Place to hammer out the details, and a document was eventually endorsed in 1982 at the TUC and Labour Party conferences.

This document pledges Labour's full support for a programme of electrification and modernization of the main lines; the replacement of rolling stock and equipment; and an increase in Freightliner and Speedlink facilities to attract freight traffic. But above all, the new policy envisages the creation of a National Transport Authority as a planning agency for the nation's transport system. At last this puts some substance into the familiar demands for an integrated system.

All I can say is, we must wait and see. My experience of the battle to win the argument over the need for the railways which we had to fight between 1975 and 1978 suggests that we must remain alert so that a future Labour Government does not backtrack on its policy commitments to the industry.

Living with Livingstone

I also have in mind what happened with the Greater London Council under Ken Livingstone in 1981. Before the local elections, the NUR had persuaded the London Labour Party to abandon its free fares policy for London Transport because we believed it was unworkable. The alternative course of action we proposed was that of reducing the fares and investing more in London Transport to provide a more frequent and reliable bus and Underground service.

Early in 1981 the NUR decided to run a campaign to be launched during the run-up to the GLC election and based on our new approach to London Transport's problems. We believed that the Underground had suffered from a deliberate policy of financial strangulation, and our aim was to bring back some sanity into the arena before it was too late.

The Underground is a good system but it is unable to operate efficiently without adequate financial provision. We wanted a strategy that would involve financial support, cuts in fares and increased use by passengers. That is why we called for an immediate reduction in fares followed by a four-year freeze. During our campaign we published a series of leaflets explaining our policy which were distributed on the Underground. We drew

58

particular attention to the Paris Metro system, acknowledged as the best in the world and far superior to the London Underground, because in the 1970s the French spent four times the amount that London Transport was able to spend during the same period.

Indeed, since 1970 more money had been poured into Paris's public transport system than into the whole of Britain's railways. In real terms the average journey in Paris cost half as much as it had twenty years before, and the system was carrying 20 per cent more passengers than five years previously.

We believed that lessons could be learned from the Paris experience. We made no apology for the timing of our campaign because we wanted Labour to capture London's County Hall to put our policy into practice. I believe that we made a crucial contribution to Labour's victory. It cost the union £20,000.

During our efforts Ken Livingstone, who was then Labour's transport spokesman, was hardly ever out of our office. He knew full well we were on to an election winner. What I didn't realize was that he planned to take over the Labour leadership on the GLC in a hard-Left coup.

As soon as he was installed in County Hall, I insisted on meeting him to discuss the implementation of the transport policy we had been advocating. After some difficulty we met on 12 May 1981. I was accompanied by Charlie Turnock, the officer responsible for London Transport. Livingstone had at least half a dozen colleagues with him.

It was a short and friendly meeting. I simply asked that before the Council made any decision on transport policy he would consult the NUR to establish priorities with us on, for example, fare reductions and levels of investment, together with pay levels, over which we were having a problem at that time with London Transport management. Livingstone readily agreed.

He then seemed to forget all about it. We never had any discussion at all on transport priorities with him, and in order to force a pay settlement out of London Transport we had to threaten to take industrial action. Indeed, Charlie Turnock tried repeatedly to reach him by telephone but without success. Livingstone was either never there or was and never rang back – it was as if he had gone off to China.

Under Livingstone the GLC seems to be more interested in political warfare with the Tory government and embarrassing the Labour Party leadership than in running transport in the capital.

Instead of a balanced approach to these problems, all that came out was a total concentration on fare cuts, with resulting political controversy and neglect of investment and pay. The disastrous effects on London's transport of the subsequent court case and yo-yoing fares is known to all.

The lesson I learned from this was that no industry, whether it is a small concern employing a handful of workers or a vast organization like the railways employing thousands, can succeed without a sense of shared purpose and a clearly defined set of objectives. Our neighbours in France have learned that lesson, but we sadly still have not.

The pay train farce

Even during Labour's years of office we were plagued by industrial conflict on the railways, which inhibited progress. The story of the pay train guards between 1977 and 1979 is a good example of the way in which inter-union conflict has in recent years paralysed developments in the railway network. Since then matters have only got worse.

The origins of this complex dispute lay in the review carried out of the industry's wages structure in 1974 before I became General Secretary. A principal feature of that exercise was to consolidate bonus and mileage payments of railwaymen into their basic rates, and this included the commission received by pay train guards. Those guards who were collecting money and selling tickets on the rural services didn't like to see their commission being consolidated because they believed that the payment was an extra for carrying out duties which were not normal for them. McCarthy's Tribunal did not support them, but the problem remained. A working party was set up to consider the reintroduction of some form of payment for the guards.

But then in August 1975 ASLEF stepped into the dispute. Ray Buckton wrote to the Railways Board and told them that if any new bonus payments went to the guards, his union would demand parallel improvements in pay and conditions for their footplate staff. He threatened that ASLEF would take industrial action to maintain the status of his men in the cab if it became necessary. By this stage many of the pay train guards were becoming increasingly angry, and some of them were refusing to take out their ticket machines as a protest.

The row dragged on until 8 February 1978, when a deal was

finally reached with the Railways Board. Management agreed to pay commission to the guards for collecting, examining and issuing tickets on rural routes. It had taken nearly three years to settle the issue and I have no doubt the main cause of that delay stemmed from ASLEF's strike threat.

Only six days after we had concluded the deal for the pay train guards, Buckton wrote to the Railways Board and demanded similar money for his members on a pro-rata basis, even though there was nothing comparable in their situation. When management did not immediately agree, he and his Executive decided to call a one-day stoppage on 1 March 1978, with further regional stoppages in Scotland on 7 March and London Midland on 9 March. Len Murray then intervened to try and settle the issue and as a result we all agreed on 28 February to put the problem before Lord McCarthy and his Tribunal colleagues, sitting as an independent inquiry team outside the railway industry bargaining structure.

On 30 March 1978 the McCarthy inquiry reported that ASLEF's claim should be put into the machinery of negotiation and treated as a matter of priority at the various stages so that it could be considered by the Railway Staff National Tribunal with the minimum of delay. The next day Buckton wrote to the Railways Board with a modified demand: that his members on the footplate should receive extra money instead as recognition for their increased productivity and responsibility.

The basis of their claim had changed because ASLEF knew full well that they had no chance of convincing anybody that a payment to a handful of pay train guards could justify similar treatment being given to all their members. We estimated that a mere 800 out of around 12,000 guards working for British Rail in any one day would get the commission, perhaps no more than 1,600 guards altogether. However, ASLEF was determined to keep up the pressure as their claim was processed through the industry's conciliation machinery. Buckton wrote to the Railways Board again and threw down an ultimatum: strike action would start on 20 July unless the McCarthy Tribunal met on 19 July to consider their demand.

I believe the ASLEF Executive was simply making mischief. It wanted to find a way to break the Social Contract pay policy. In doing so it was mixing the case of the pay train guards with a totally different issue: that of overall productivity payments. This went back to September 1977 when we had approached the Railways Board with the suggestion that it might be possible to devise a genuine, self-financing productivity deal for railwaymen which would provide them with extra money on top of the 10 per cent pay guidelines. In January 1978 my union sent details of what we had in mind to British Rail for them to look at. We thought that any scheme should be designed to provide weekly payments to cover all railwaymen, not a chosen few. It was suggested that a suitable index of performance could be established to measure the productivity of the system by using freight tonne miles plus passenger miles to be divided by either the number of staff employed or by the total hours worked.

Such a scheme had the clear advantage that it could start at once if it was based on a year-by-year comparison over a representative period of time to be decided upon. The plan required a joint union-management effort, and it was not to be used simply as a device to cut manpower. The NUR had always taken the view that the best way to improve productivity was to increase the use of the railway network. British Rail came up with a scheme that met most of the principles which we had set out, but ASLEF insisted that their members were entitled to a separate productivity scheme and they opposed the national incentive plan.

The Board then made it clear that unless all the unions agreed there would be no productivity deal for anybody. It seemed to me that the ASLEF leaders were blocking our talks on a national productivity scheme until they had made out their own case to the McCarthy Tribunal for special treatment for their footplate staff in line with the pay train guards. In these absurd circumstances, the Board then said it was going to refer the whole question to McCarthy to sort out.

In our evidence to the resulting Tribunal hearing I made it clear that the NUR was not opposed to footplate staff getting higher rewards for greater productivity, but we did reject the idea that footplate staff alone were a special case or had made a bigger contribution to improving productivity in the industry than any other staff. It was ridiculous to isolate the contribution of one group of railway workers in working out a reward. How could any single grade claim improved productivity which stemmed from electrification, resignalling and higher speeds? The way to reward staff for greater effort was through a national scheme where everybody played their part and everybody was paid some extra money.

I told the Tribunal that to attempt to isolate one group of railwaymen from the rest was divisive and would turn the railway network into a battlefield. As I saw it, additional responsibility and the acceptance of changed technology could be met by a reclassification of those directly affected into higher, better-paid grades. We ha . enjoyed some success in doing this for the signalmen and track staff, both of whom had shown greater readiness to accept change than the train drivers.

The Tribunal's own conclusions mostly supported our case. McCarthy and his colleagues could find no justification for a separate payment to footplate grades on grounds of productivity, but they did suggest that those driving trains at more than 100 miles an hour were justified in some extra money equal to 25 per cent of the basic rate per turn per driver (£3.14 per turn). A month later the Tribunal gave its conclusions on the national productivity scheme proposal. It recommended an overall plan that would apply to all grades on the basis of a common formula. McCarthy and his colleagues did not accept the sectionalist arguments of ASLEF, pointing out that 'a properly designed scheme of this kind would be rather less divisive than a series of sectional claims and counter-claims which were lodged on behalf of different grades and groups.'

But the ASLEF Executive rejected the award and demanded an immediate meeting with the Railways Board where it said that it would be seeking a 'satisfactory offer' from the Board in response to their claim, which turned out to be a rise of 25 per cent for all drivers. The Board turned this down flat and suggested a working party to examine agreements and working practices relative to footplate staff to see whether their productivity and effectiveness could be increased and consequently rewarded. On 24 November 1978 ASLEF accepted the idea but warned that if the final report did not satisfy the union, there would be a dispute.

On 29 November Buckton set a deadline: an agreement must be reached by 7 January 1979. I protested against the continued short-sightedness of the train drivers and described their union as a rogue elephant trampling over the industry.

At the same meeting working parties had been established to consider salaried staff and other groups. We made it clear to the Board that all these working parties must run in parallel with the wide terms of reference settled for the footplatemen. The NUR would not be dragged about by a handful of drivers.

63

ASLEF at early meetings had demanded a 10 per cent pay rise for its members, but the Board made it clear that it would not start any payments unless there were corresponding improvements in productivity.

At a subsequent meeting on 10 January 1979 it became clear to me that the Railways Board planned to abandon the national productivity scheme in favour of individual working parties who would quantify productivity savings for each group of staff. Each group would then have to report back to the negotiators to decide how those savings might be shared out.

My Executive met the following day. We decided that the future of the national productivity scheme should be a matter for negotiation at the end of its first year of operation, and not simply dropped in favour of separate productivity talks with different sections of railway staff. However, we did allow individual working parties to go on so that at least we could see the scope of the productivity savings that were possible, but we wanted to make it quite clear that these matters were separate and distinct from the 1979 wages settlement. ASLEF then turned up the heat again by telling the Board that unless satisfactory progress was made by 12 January, the union's members would strike on 16 and 18 January.

On 12 January the Railways Board negotiators presented what they had in mind for proposed productivity improvements to footplate staff. This involved the loss of around 1,500 jobs. British Rail suggested that guards should also agree to a package of changes including the elimination of mileage payments, the introduction of driver-only operation for suburban trains equipped with sliding doors, and for freight train guards to do care and maintenance work. There was to be a reduction in the number of signalmen in boxes. A new grade of 'stationman' was to be introduced on stations to enable them to be covered by one man on split shifts or with part-time staff. In total, the Board estimated its proposals would mean a cut of 20,000 to 25,000 jobs on the network.

There was nothing new about these proposals. British Rail had produced them in their 1976 document, *Opportunity for Change*. I thought it was quite intolerable that these issues were being raised, at that moment, just because ASLEF continued to demand special treatment for footplate staff. Our policies were clear enough. We were not in the business of trading jobs for productivity. We were actually asking British Rail to fill 10,000 vacancies which existed, and we wanted to see cuts in excessive overtime working. The right way forward was to reward efficiency through a national scheme and not by sectionalist deals.

With the deadline of the ASLEF strike fast approaching, the Transport Minister, who was then Bill Rodgers, had us all in to see him, trying to find a way out of the crisis. On 17 January the Railways Board suggested that the unions should process their pay claims as quickly as possible by bringing all the working parties together, including footplatemen, salaried staffs and the conciliators. They were to go into continuous session to see what productivity improvements could be agreed and how much money they might generate. We agreed to this but ASLEF refused.

I was having none of this, and the whole messy business was referred back to McCarthy and his colleagues for their final verdict. In April 1979 the Tribunal rejected the demand of the drivers for a 10 per cent bonus, but they did agree that the drivers should get a 5 per cent 'responsibility allowance', so their antics paid off.

This sorry tale shows just how ASLEF pursued its own interests selfishly at the expense of the rest of the railway workers. Commuters were the innocent pawns in a power struggle. The Board had displayed too much patience with the ASLEF Executive. I believed that if you gave them an inch, they would take a mile. We spent months, indeed years, scrapping about the minor issue of the pay train guards, when the whole railway industry was facing a grave crisis. It was a ridiculous misuse of our time and energies. We made no friends during that marathon dispute, and no doubt we drove many customers off the railways for good. But compared to events of the next few years that little episode looks like a storm in a teacup, for ASLEF was to continue to flex its muscles and cripple the railway industry.

Thatcher and the Rail Crisis 1979-81

The Railwaymen's Charter

Mrs Thatcher's election victory in May 1979 heralded a new and bleaker age for the railway industry. It had been hard enough for us to interest Labour Ministers in the need to modernize the railway network, but now we found it even more difficult to convince the Government of the financial support we needed to keep the industry up with the times.

The Prime Minister seems to have a particular dislike for railways. She has not travelled on a train since coming to office. Nor does she have any time for the nationalized industries. So we suffered on both scores.

The unions and the Railways Board seemed to be spending more and more time trying to persuade Ministers that the industry should have a future. It turned out to be a frustrating and never-ending process, demonstrating that sheer inertia and lack of decision in government are the biggest single obstacles to making Britain a more dynamic and prosperous economy. I cannot pretend there will ever be very much common ground between the NUR and a Conservative Government. I have spent most of my life fighting the Tory party, but you have to accept it when it is elected democratically. I was always ready to talk to the Tories if only to impress on the Minister that the Government could not deny its responsibility for running the railways.

Mrs Thatcher's attempt to shake herself free from any involvement in large parts of the public sector lies at the heart of many of the problems confronting the trade unions today. I do not believe that the unions have yet fully come to terms with the fact that for the first time since the Second World War we have a Government totally hostile to the public sector.

The day-to-day reality is that each union is forced to find its own salvation according to the circumstances of the individual company or industry. The choice is often between standing by a basic political principle and the concept of State ownership or protecting jobs whatever the circumstances.

This was more than a theoretical exercise for the NUR. The Government announced the privatization of British Rail hotels. After considerable discussion with British Rail, my union reached agreement on the formation of a new company to run Gleneagles. We agreed on terms of employment and that the closed shop would continue. In return, the NUR invested £600,000 in the new company and together with British Rail we hold a 40 per cent stake in the hotel. I don't offer that as a blueprint for resolving all the problems caused to trade unions by privatization, but in a desperate last resort unions can only formulate their approach on the basis that the protection of its membership is paramount.

It was also clear to me in the early days of the Conservative Government that the unions and the Board would have to work much closer together in common cause if we were to achieve the financial assistance we needed to meet current costs and modernize the system.

Progress on ways of improving productivity had been very slow. During 1979 alone some 120,000 man days were spent in negotiations. But I was well aware that the Tories would be unready to back our demands unless we were ready to show a greater willingness to accept efficiences. My main concern was to make sure I did not concede anything that worsened the position of my members in return for nothing at all. As part of our 1979 pay deal my union gave firm commitments to have positive talks with the Railways Board on ways of increasing productivity to make the business much more competitive. But it soon became clear to me that there was a wide gulf between what the Board expected and what my union had in mind. From our point of view, it was nonsense for the Board to talk about cutting manpower when there was already a critical staff shortage in many areas, which brought train cancellations and far more overtime and rest-day working than was desirable.

I believed that the railways should be looking towards expansion, not rundown, as rocketing oil and petrol prices added to the costs of travel, but management thinking seemed to be rooted in the sixties. Their bland acceptance of a diminishing role for the railways in the freight business, for example, merely confirmed their negative approach to the future of the entire railway industry. It was clear that little progress was likely to be made unless both sides began to agree on fundamentals. So I decided that the way to break out of the deadlock was for my union to take an entirely fresh look at the problems we were faced with. All too often in the past we had seen the railway network shrinking. Successive Board Chairmen had promised to raise the living standards of railway workers in return for their co-operation in improving the efficiency of the industry. But they had not honoured what they said they would do.

Between 1966 and 1979 as many as 150,000 railway jobs had gone but my members were still lagging behind in the national wages league table. We remained inadequately rewarded for the unsocial hours worked to maintain a round-the-clock service for the general public, while we enjoyed far fewer holidays than workers in most other industries.

There were two courses of action open to us. The first and certainly the easiest for me was to simply sit back and do nothing at all. But that to me was an unrealistic strategy. Management would gradually cut down the number of staff anyway through their control of recruitment and so the many problems of my members would not be resolved. The second course – and I made no bones about the difficulties it would cause – was to square up to all the questions, sit down with management and see how far we could go towards solving them to our mutual benefit. After considerable discussion and debate I persuaded my Executive that we should seek a new deal for our membership and confront the problems facing the industry. I went along to the Rail Council with that in mind.

I found Parker in a pessimistic mood about the state of British Rail's finances. He told us that the Government was setting the industry strict financial targets which involved a ceiling on borrowing of £715 million in the 1979-80 financial year. To stay within that limit the Board was already being compelled to accelerate the sale of railway property, reduce the level of its stock holdings and increase sales of scrap materials, yet even by following this desperate course of action the Board's finances were going to stay on a knife edge and there was a real danger of the Government's limits being exceeded.

I told Parker that my union knew the problems well enough, but I warned him that my union's annual conference had made it quite clear that the NUR was not going to trade jobs for productivity. At a later meeting with the Board I spelt out the NUR's initial demand: to achieve a first-class railway system for Britain which would involve a £288 million boost in rates of pay and conditions of service for my members. This was the outline of what became the *Railwaymen's Charter*. The objective would be to create a new pay structure, a move towards a 35-hour basic working week, and four weeks' annual leave for all staff.

In exchange for those improvements, which I said were our first thoughts and not a final precise requirement, I promised Parker that we would be ready as a union to discuss the ways in which the Board wanted to improve productivity. We were willing to consider any management proposals, however radical they might turn out to be, as a quid pro quo for the better deal for railwaymen. However, unless the Board was ready to contemplate what we had in mind the position of our members would only worsen and they would therefore not co-operate in efficiency measures for small rewards.

Parker pointed out that our proposals did not really help him solve his short-term cash crisis. In the longer run the Board would have to ask the Government for more money for investment, but Ministers were hardly going to respond in a favourable fashion unless the Board could win Government confidence in the way it was tackling the current rail crisis. The kind of improvements we were after could only come with more money from the Government because not enough could be generated through genuine productivity improvements. It would be necessary to convince Ministers that in exchange for better pay and conditions of service, radical changes in labour practices would be introduced to achieve a more efficient railway network.

We knew that the Board would not be able to meet the whole of the cost of what we wanted at one go, even through a major productivity package. I saw that there must be a phased timetable for achievement. This meant a joint approach from the unions and the Board to ask for the money needed as the price that would have to be paid for a future railway which would be productive.

As a result of that discussion my union research department

drew up our main aims. These were to give a first priority to a substantial increase in basic wage rates for all grades with a structure which would range from £60 to £100 a week for conciliation staff and from £4,500 to £6,500 a year for supervisors and appropriate adjustments to clerical salaries. On top of this, improved payments were to be made for irregular and unsocial hours of working, a shorter working week, four weeks' annual leave, protection of earnings by indexation against inflation, firm guarantees that no jobs would be lost, a commitment to maintaining the existing railway network; and the abandonment of any plans to substitute rail services with buses.

These proposals formed our *Railwaymen's Charter*. While the TSSA backed our approach, I am afraid to say that ASLEF would not and this made it very difficult to make any progress at all.

For their part, the Board laid out what they wanted from the rail unions in a document entitled *The Challenge of the Eighties*. This suggested that as many as 30,000 jobs would have to go over the next three years, one in six of the entire labour force. British Rail laid out what they wanted to see happen, with sweeping changes in manpower practices. Among other things this meant closing old marshalling yards and running down the collection and delivery of parcels.

The most radical proposals concerned the operation and manning of trains. The Board wanted to see what it called 'flexibility in the provision of freight services' through 'greater adaptability to changing workloads'. A new 'trainman' was to be introduced to replace the traditional conductor and guard. Mention was made of flexible rostering so that Saturdays and Sundays were included in the standard week instead of being overtime working.

Talks were so lengthy on these issues that they ran into our 1980 pay claim negotiations. The Board was keen to establish a linkage in the 1980 negotiations between productivity improvements and wage rises, but we resisted this, arguing that the two issues should be kept separate. The three rail unions came together with a joint pay claim and agreed to co-ordinate our efforts and stick together. This was the first time in living memory that we had found common cause in the annual wage negotiations, and I made it clear to the Board that if any industrial action was necessary to further our demand we would act as one.

The Board started by offering us an overall 13 per cent increase in basic rates, with a further 4 per cent to come from productivity improvements, but we were determined to get a better deal. Negotiations were to prove relatively trouble-free in 1980 despite the difficulties of the railway industry and we eventually arrived at a deal without, as so often before, having to troop off to the McCarthy Tribunal. In the negotiations a two-part pay offer made by the Board was rejected by the NUR Executive by a decisive 21 votes to 6, and the Board eventually agreed to pay us a full 20 per cent increase in one go without strings on 5 May 1980. It cost them £220 million and pushed up the basic minimum earnings to £66.60 a week outside London, while the basic rates of higher-class signalmen and engine drivers went over £100 a week for the first time.

The Board also agreed to cut the basic working week from 40 to 39 hours in November 1981 and improved staff holidays for those with two years' service. In the harsh political climate in which we were forced to negotiate in 1980 and against the background of the Board's tight financial position, the achievement of 20 per cent was a real success and it demonstrated the value of having a unified approach by all three rail unions in wage negotiations.

But we did agree to co-operate, as part of the deal, in certain changes that the Board had sought to implement. The 1980 pay agreement committed us to consult and implement the rationalization of the freight marshalling yards and collection and delivery of parcels. We also accepted further talks on ways of rationalizing the freight and parcels business as well as of streamlining the administration. Discussions were to continue on the changes in working practices that the Board had spelt out in *Challenge of the Eighties*.

I had high hopes that we would be able to make some real progress in matching improved pay and conditions with increased efficiency. But in the summer of 1980 the economic recession began to hit British Rail's finances sharply. There was a sharp fall in passenger traffic and a deterioration in the freight and parcels service. The Board decided to try and remedy the difficulties by cutting back on its investment programme and banning all recruitment except to fill essential vacancies. For our part, we decided to clarify the objectives set out in the *Railwaymen's Charter*, calling for security of employment, improved basic wage rates to make sure our members stayed in line with comparable workers in outside industries, moves to a 35-hour basic week over a five-year period, a simplified shift system of working, and moves on improved holidays to achieve a five-week holiday in the near future.

I realized that what we were asking for would be expensive and not to be achieved overnight, but I re-emphasized that our acceptance of more discussions on changes in business and working practices had been made on the clear understanding that further improvements would come in the pay and conditions of my members. I had hoped the other two rail unions would join us in our proposals, but they would not, so I decided that the NUR should try and go it alone with the Board. However, the Board refused to respond to my approach because of the negative attitude of the other unions. I pointed out to the Board the value to both of us of our radical proposals, and told them that the other unions would eventually be forced to follow, but by this stage the industry's crisis was worsening rapidly and events overtook us.

The Watford crisis summit

Parker spelt out the gravity of the rail crisis at a summit conference held at The Grove, British Rail's training college at Watford, on 19 and 20 November 1980. He told us that the industry could not go to the Government with a begging bowl. We must show what we could do ourselves. He saw the alternatives as either tackling British Rail's troubles constructively or slogging it out in trench warfare. The slump was now hitting both the passenger and freight side of the business and the Board's financial position was deteriorating rapidly. Parker told us all that the option of doing nothing was not open to the Board.

I had no doubt that Parker found himself in a difficult position. The External Financing Limit (EFL) – the total amount of money the Board could receive from outside its own resources with Government authority – was going to overshoot in that financial year by between £25 million and £45 million, and he reckoned it would need a 30 per cent increase in EFL to £972 million in 1981-82 if the industry was to avoid a serious decline in its services.

Parker left us in no doubt at all that we would have no chance of persuading Ministers to accept that kind of rise in the present tight financial conditions. Norman Fowler, the Minister of Transport, had already agreed to extend the present year's EFL from £750 million to £790 million only on the understanding that British Rail's future investment proposals would be examined in the light of what the industry had done to improve its own efficiency.

Apparently the Minister was sitting on £400 million worth of new projects, including new rolling stock and a £56.5 million electrification programme for the East Anglia line.

Parker told us that the Board believed it could cut down its needs for a larger EFL to £892 million through changes in business operations and the selling off of some of its property assets. But even if he managed to win Fowler's approval for the bigger EFL he wanted, the Board would still need between £25 million and £45 million to take account of the year's overspending, and a further £50 million would be needed in temporary borrowing.

This was the background against which Parker asked all three rail unions to join him in signing a 'balance sheet of change'. The idea was that the Board and the rail unions together would co-operate in a number of adjustments. These involved an acceleration in the rundown of obsolete marshalling yards, the withdrawal from the collection and delivery of parcels, a cut of 5 per cent in passenger train mileage, a streamlining of administration to save money and the promise of continuing support from the unions in what the Board called 'good housekeeping'.

Parker also wanted us to agree to an early meeting of the industry's negotiating machinery to review progress on the commitments contained in the 1980 wage agreement over changes in working practices, so that decisions could be made on them by March 1981 at the latest. What particularly concerned the Board was to achieve a breakthrough on single manning on motive power traction units, and the recruitment and training of traincrew staff. It also wanted to develop the 'open station' concept, whereby passengers would buy their tickets on board the train, leaving stations unmanned. Parker argued that if we could deliver on those proposals, as we had already promised to do, then he could ask Fowler with more confidence to make an early decision on the Advanced Passenger Train, 'jumbo' ferries, East Anglia electrification and new rolling stock.

Without agreement being reached, he warned, the industry was heading fast for what he called 'Operation Plughole'. The crunch year was 1983. I told Parker that I would place the terms of what we had discussed before my Executive Committee, but I emphasized that I was not ready at that stage to say whether I would recommend what he wanted. My Executive had asked for the facts and the alternatives and it would be up to them to decide what our policy ought to be.

Even before my Executive met to consider what to do, Fowler announced that the Board's EFL for the next financial year was to be £867 million, £25 million less than the Board's own estimated need. I realized as a result of the Watford conference that the only way we could solve our problems was by the Government, the Railways Board and the rail unions reaching some sort of common strategy.

The unions had to present a policy which would set out clearly how they saw the creation of a railway system providing a service to the nation in the efficient movement of people and freight, and the acceptance of new technologies and work practices which would make this possible.

I saw our *Railwaymen's Charter* and the 'balance sheet of change' hammered out at Watford as part of those policies. What we required was the necessary commitment from each of the partners – the Government, the Board and the unions. If we all delivered our side of a national bargain for the future of the industry, I believed that we could make some real progress. After two days of intense debate I persuaded my Executive of the merit of that kind of strategy. They agreed unanimously with the 'balance sheet of change' approach, but also demanded an urgent meeting with Fowler to discuss the rail crisis.

On 29 January 1981 all the unions on the Rail Council went to see Fowler at his Department in Marsham Street. Parker told him that we had agreed on a 'balance sheet of change' but in return we wanted the Government to give the railway industry a much more positive and broader perspective for the future with the promise of more investment for key projects, a rise in British Rail's investment ceiling and increased subsidies for unprofitable lines. He told Fowler in no uncertain terms that the railways faced a crisis and 1983 would be the crucial year.

I was equally blunt. I told Fowler that I profoundly disagreed with the Government on many issues and I would like to see the back of them as soon as possible, but he was the Transport Minister and I had to live with him, so we had to see whether we could at least come to an understanding for the good of the industry.

I spelt out what my union wanted to see happen. We favoured an increase in the Board's EFL to £970 million, increased support for passenger services, an extension of Government backing for freight operations and the early go-ahead for electrification schemes and new rolling stock. If the Government came up with the necessary cash to meet the Board's needs, I said, we were ready to co-operate with an acceleration in the closure of the marshalling yards and the withdrawal of the collection and delivery of parcels that would save the industry £50 million. But I added that further efficiencies that the Board wanted would have to come through the industry's own negotiating machinery. Men who lose their jobs because of changes should be able to be redeployed elsewhere in the industry. However, I assured him that we would try to settle those difficulties over working practices by 31 March at the latest, as the Board was demanding.

We emphasized that we thought it was quite unacceptable that all the gestures of goodwill should come from the rail unions, and urged that Fowler must take an initiative in return. He seemed to be saying that if improvements were made in the industry, then the Government would help out, but I warned him that a promise from Ministers about what they might do in response to initiatives from the railwaymen was not good enough, because it was too vague.

I made it clear that we needed to 'synchronize' the commitments on both sides, because I had real doubts whether my union would be willing to deliver for its part if the Government's commitment for the future remained so imprecise.

Fowler told us it had been a useful and important meeting, and he thought a joint approach to resolve British Rail's problems between the Board and the unions would help him in his discussions inside the Cabinet with his less sympathetic colleagues on the Board's plans and its demand for the green light on electrification. Apparently he recognized that the timing of decisions was all-important and he said he would be quite happy to continue the dialogue that had started. Fowler admitted 'there was a need for a sensible bipartisan programme.' It was agreed that we should all meet again in June to review what progress had been made.

The Watford summit conference and the meeting with Fowler gave me some hope that we might at last achieve a breakthrough to a greater understanding with Government on what the industry needed. For his part, Parker decided to keep up the pressure by publishing in March his document *Rail Policy*, which set out policy aims and the potential of the industry for the eighties. He put the problem in stark language that everybody could understand: 'BR must prepare to take either the path of progress by re-equipment and modernization or that of decline through a gradual but de-

75

liberate rundown of the system. We cannot continue as we have done in the past. We are reaching the dividing of the ways.'

The document laid out the strategy for the future: the arrival of the Advanced Passenger Train; the electrification of the main lines; the creation of a Channel rail tunnel; a cross-London north-to-south rail link; a huge investment in new rolling stock, tracks and signalling. There was to be a new deal for the South-East commuters and an expansion in business for Freightliner and Speedlink.

In a section entitled, 'A Productive and Committed Workforce' it also had some words of praise for railwaymen: 'The high morale and dedication to work, which is linked to our successes in the past, is the key factor in keeping the railways running. We know that hourly pay is relatively low, that in a 24-hour business many have to work unsocial hours, that many have to work in the open in all weathers. We owe all these people our thanks and gratitude.' Parker's plan recognized a problem that I had been raising for some time: the large numbers of railway workers who were leaving the industry and the very short time that many recruits stayed. It admitted that there were indeed 'acute shortages in certain grades'. The document even acknowledged the demands of my union's *Railwaymen's Charter*, saying that it was time for a 'new deal' for the staff. 'Decent working facilities for our staff have too often been left until last or not provided at all,' it admitted. 'Too many carriages still have to be cleaned and maintained in the open air.'

I had high hopes that the Government would move in British Rail's direction. A joint British Railways Board-Department of Transport study backed the electrification plans in February 1981, and this seemed to suggest we should have few problems in winning Cabinet backing for the go-ahead. But through the spring and early summer of 1981 no signs came out of the Department of Transport that Fowler was ready to deliver his side of the 'balance sheet of change' we had all talked so grandly about in January. It looked as though our good intentions were failing to make any impact where it mattered.

On 22 June, as agreed, Fowler met the Rail Council to tell us of the decisions he had reached as a consequence of our January discussion. He told us that the Government intended to demonstrate its intention of securing the future of the railways and that it was ready to agree on a ten-year electrification programme. In the short run he agreed to increase the external financing limit for the present financial year. He recognized what had been achieved in the rail industry over the past twelve months, but he kept on stressing that it was only if we could satisfy him and his Cabinet colleagues that the railways were doing all in their power to help themselves would he be able to argue for increased investment. Fowler argued that carriage and freight should not have to be subsidized and that the Inter-City service should be made into a commercial business. On electrification, he suggested that the Government would approve individual schemes each year but also look for some real progress on productivity and business performance. Fowler indicated that he wanted to see the Board's 1981-85 corporate plan carried through, with a cut of 38,000 in the workforce over the period.

I was not very satisfied by what I heard, particularly the staff cuts, and I told Fowler that I found difficulty in evaluating just what the Government was doing. I believed it was essential that we should all be clear about Government policy, because otherwise it would be extremely difficult to convince railwaymen that the Minister had really picked up his fair share of the problems. The Government was adopting double standards, for while the coal industry had recently received massive financial aid, the railways were getting quite different and most unfavourable treatment. I asked Fowler whether, in demanding greater productivity, he was aware of the decision by British Rail Engineering (BREL) to close down its Ashford works in Kent and put the rest of its workforce on a four-day week, at a time when the industry was desperately short of rolling stock and other vital equipment. To a large extent this had been brought about by inadequate investment in the industry, and by his failure to give the Board the go-ahead for their plans.

The other unions echoed my disappointment. Parker drew Fowler's attention to what the NUR had achieved over the past year in rationalization of working practices. A further meeting on productivity was due on 14 and 15 July 1981 in the hope of a significant breakthrough. Parker told Fowler that the Board was in a position to respond at once on a ten-year electrification programme and he reminded the Minister that details of the East Anglia scheme had been with his Department for some time. In presenting a line-by-line electrification plan Parker welcomed the opportunity this gave the industry to redefine its purpose on the Inter-City routes.

But all of us on the Rail Council made it clear that we did not think the Government had made an adequate response at all in the key areas on the 'balance sheet of change', especially on investment in new rolling stock. We had begun to deliver our part of the bargain we had agreed last winter, but the Government so far had made only a very limited response. Fowler, in reply, stressed that he would like to hang on to a phrase Parker has used: 'The railway industry has not lost.' He repeated that the Government were experiencing difficulties with public spending, but he assured us that there should be no misunderstanding, for the Government had accepted the benefits of electrification provided it was justified by the Board's business performance.

The rail unions met the Board for further talks on the 'balance sheet of change' in July 1981. Parker and his colleagues told us that whatever the financial framework for the industry might be, progress on productivity was an integral part of British Rail's future. Ministers were expecting to see some positive action on the areas of efficiency laid out in *Challenge of the Eighties*, such as the manning of trains, flexible rostering, and the 'open station' concept. These vexed questions became tied up in our difficult pay negotiations that summer.

At first, it didn't look as though the growing rail crisis over pay and productivity was hardening attitudes in the Cabinet. In September 1981 Fowler was transferred to the Department of Health and Social Security and he was replaced at Transport by David Howell. I was desperately waiting for a meeting with the new Minister and hoping for some firm statement of Government intentions when the Rail Council met him for the first time at Marsham Street on 17 December.

Howell assured us that he wanted to see a flourishing, well-invested railway industry and he said he saw this as essential for Britain's future. He told us categorically that he did not want to see any substantial cuts in the size of the existing rail network and he agreed that the Government had a large part to play in resolving the problems of the South-East commuter routes. To show his good will he had agreed to an increase in the Board's EFL for 1982-83 to £950 million. Howell went on to talk – as Fowler had done before him – of synchronizing Government backing for programmes of electrification with productivity improvements. He said he was now ready to consider the East Anglia electrification scheme in advance of the main programme.

The official report of that crucial Rail Council meeting says that the Government was willing to go along with my approach. Howell even recognized that there had been movement by the railways on the 'balance sheet of change'. I told him that it was essential that we carried the workforce with us in accepting change and this would become increasingly difficult if the Government gave no sign that it was ready to meet its commitments. I urged him to give the go-ahead to East Anglia electrification as quickly as possible. Time was running out for the Government and a decision was needed on that project within weeks. The unions and British Rail pressed Howell for a further meeting within six weeks to see what progress had been made. Under pressure the Minister agreed to a further meeting within that time, in January 1982. He added that he hoped to give the go-ahead to the East Anglia scheme in the near future. In fact, he announced his decision on that electrification programme in the House of Commons just before Christmas, at the same time as I signed the flexible rostering agreement for the NUR.

I was quite pleased at the outcome of the December meeting with Howell and I fully expected an early decision in January to electrify the East Coast line from King's Cross to Newcastle. But even as we were talking the industry was fast entering its worst crisis for more than twenty years. There had been no mention at Marsham Street of the lengthy discussions on productivity that had been going on through the autumn. 'Flexible rostering' had not yet hit the headlines.

In December 1981 we stood a good chance of winning the Government's backing for the future of the industry. Progress had proved painfully slow and the recession and tight financial restrictions by the Treasury had played havoc with British Rail's aims. But because of the strength of our case which we had jointly presented during the whole of 1981, I had a reasonable hope that in 1982 we would make the breakthrough. The Government seemed on the point of backing the 10-year electrification programme. But when we were so near success, disaster struck in the shape of industrial conflict on the railways. The resulting mayhem put paid to all my hopes and continues to jeopardize the entire future of the network.

The Strikes of 1982

To the brink

The industrial crisis on the railways in 1981-82 inflicted grave damage on the system and put into severe doubt the Government's commitment to preserve the present network intact, let alone modernize it. My hopes of a breakthrough were dashed by the irresponsible behaviour of ASLEF over flexible rostering. The start of our troubles really came in the summer of 1981 when we were driven to the brink of an all-out strike, and from then on my in-tray seemed constantly to fill up with one problem after another.

I submitted a claim for a substantial pay rise for my members on 11 February 1981. We needed an increase on basic wage rates of at least 13 per cent to keep up with the rate of inflation and ensure no further fall in living standards. It took over two months for the Board to come up with an offer of 7 per cent from 20 April 1981, which we found totally unsatisfactory. The Board refused to improve the offer at further negotiating sessions, so my Executive Committee decided to take the claim to the McCarthy Tribunal for adjudication.

I had begun to feel that British Rail was posturing as a 'good employer' while hiding behind the industry's financial position to avoid fulfilling their commitment to better pay and conditions. Their attitude was breeding resentment and frustration among my members who saw their living standards falling. 'The current situation has all the ingredients of a major industrial dispute in the railway industry,' I told the Tribunal. Government failure to provide enough money for investment was making it harder day by day for my members to cope with the problems of operating clapped-out and antiquated equipment and at the same time providing an adequate service for the public.

The Board argued before McCarthy that its finances were being stretched to offer even 7 per cent and the Government would have to be asked to provide further bridging aid to meet its cash needs. But in its award the Tribunal made some substantial improvement to British Rail's offer. It took the form of a two-stage increase for all railwaymen. An 8 per cent rise was to be backdated to 20 April and a further increase of 3 per cent was to be paid from 1 August. This would add a further £50 million to British Rail's pay bill.

After much heated argument the Board announced it was not going to honour the Tribunal award unless the rail unions agreed to commit themselves to specific productivity improvements drawn from the Board's earlier document, *Challenge of the Eighties*. I warned Parker that the industry would be at the barricades if he did not agree to the McCarthy award. The Tribunal had made thirty awards during my years as General Secretary and some of them I had not liked, but I had accepted them. I told him to look at the fine print of the award because it had taken into account progress we had made on productivity.

But Parker dug in his heels, saying he would only pay out the 3 per cent to us if we agreed to sweeping changes in manpower practices. I saw his problem, and I did not want to have an industrial confrontation if this could be avoided. I drew up a paper which set out what the union would be prepared to do, in the spirit of our 1979 *Railwaymen's Charter*, but my Executive Committee would not let me present this to the Board, insisting that all 11 per cent of the McCarthy award must be honoured without any strings attached.

In further talks on 3 August Parker presented us with a six-point programme of efficiency proposals. These included fewer men in the cabs of freight and passenger trains, flexible rostering, 'open' stations and the easing of manning levels on one-man operated trains. The Board insisted we must accept those reforms in order to get the extra 3 per cent. Our talks collapsed and I could see we were heading into the first national rail strike for half a century.

My Executive and that of ASLEF issued notice that an all-out stoppage would start on 31 August. By announcing almost a month's notice we were giving the Board and the Government time to find a way out.

On 18 August the independent Advisory Conciliation and Arbitration Service (ACAS) intervened to try and break the deadlock. It was to take four days of exhausting talks at ACAS headquarters before we reached an agreement on the pay and productivity issues. The unions sat in one room, the Board in another, with Pat Lowry, Chairman of ACAS, as go-between. ACAS officials like to keep everybody in their building to speed up the resolving of disputes, but I became so fed up with eating sandwiches and fish and chips round the clock that I insisted on going off for a hot meal in a restaurant with my NUR colleagues.

The Board insisted on a timetable of commitments on productivity in the six areas where they wanted progress before they would agree to pay the extra 3 per cent of the McCarthy award. They wanted cast-iron guarantees that we would deliver on all the items within the time proposed.

The talks almost broke down when Parker demanded a much more precise form of words to cover each of the six productivity commitments than I believed was necessary. I told Lowry that we had gone far enough in trying to reach a settlement and I was doing no more. The NUR was ready to honour the agreement to the letter but the Board wanted too firm a commitment. 'Don't go carrying any more messages to them from me', I said to Lowry. 'I am going to tell them myself. If these six points I have agreed to are not acceptable to the Board, there will be nobody working from 31 August.' It was agreed by the other union leaders that I should act as spokesman.

We went down the corridor to the room where the Board leaders were sitting and Lowry told them I had something to say. I made it clear that all three rail union leaders were ready to honour to the letter the understandings on pay and productivity, and to persuade their Executives to accept them. Even at that late stage, the Board leaders argued and haggled, but they came round to accepting they had got the best they could in the circumstances.

What surprises me in retrospect is that flexible rostering was not seen as important during those marathon ACAS talks. We spent about five minutes talking about the issue, and Ray Buckton and his President Bill Ronksley did not raise a murmur to suggest that it might create any difficulties. On the other hand, the discussions nearly collapsed over the much more important issues of the manning of freight trains and the role of the guards on the new Bedford-London St Pancras electrified commuter service.

Under the ACAS agreement, British Rail agreed to pay in January 1982 the 3 per cent backdated to August on top of the 8 per cent they had already accepted. For our part, we accepted a postponement from October until January of the cut of one hour in the basic working week from 40 to 39 hours. But under the productivity understanding which accompanied the pay formula, we also agreed to enter serious negotiations on achieving a settlement by specific dates. We agreed in principle to the 'open station' concept. Negotiations were to be finished with a 'basis for agreement by 31 October 1981'.

On the manning of the Bedford-St Pancras line discussions were to take place 'without any preconceived conditions on either side' and no deadline for a deal was laid down. Negotiations were going to be completed by 31 October 1981 on single manning on traction units as long as appropriate safety measures had been agreed and there was no worsening of staff conditions. An 'immediate joint examination' was to be set up on manning freight trains without guards and 'two or three pilot schemes' were to start on this by 1 January 1982 'if possible'. Negotiations were also to be finished by the same date on the 'trainman' concept.

On flexible rostering, the wording of the understanding was quite clear. It said: 'Negotiations shall take place to establish variations to the rostering agreements with a view to introducing some flexibility around the eight-hour day but without producing unreasonable variation in the length of each working day or week. These discussions shall be concluded by 31 October 1981.'

The document I signed along with Buckton and Tom Jenkins of the TSSA for the unions contained assurances from all of us that we would 'honour every aspect of the understanding reached on productivity'. The two understandings reached at ACAS on pay and productivity were separate from each other but they were also linked together. Without the commitment by the Board to implement the McCarthy award we would not have reached a settlement at ACAS, but equally I am sure the Board would never have signed the deal if Parker had not believed that the rail unions would all deliver in full the productivity commitments they had signed.

There was no fudge here. It was clear to me that the agreement on flexible rosters meant that the working day for railwaymen

83

would vary around the eight-hour day, and that this could mean fewer hours as well as more being worked.

The rostering crisis begins

Through the autumn of 1981 we held long negotiations on the productivity commitments. Progress proved painfully slow on most of them. Eight separate meetings were held on the issue of flexible rostering for the footplate staff, but there was no break-through. However, it was not until mid-November that Buckton made it fully clear that his Executive was opposed totally to any change in the basic eight-hour working day. I learned that in fact Buckton had been rebuffed by the ASLEF Executive up at Arkwright Road when the ink was hardly dry on the August understandings. They then went through a charade of pretending to negotiate on the issue. Russell Tuck, who led our team of negotiators, had been talking in good faith with the Board, but we were participating in a pointless rigmarole while the ASLEF leaders were simply going through the motions of discussion and had made up their minds already.

By December we had negotiated successfully a flexible rostering agreement for all railway staff, including guards – except for the footplatemen. Never in my career had I signed any agreements for NUR members that made their working life worse, and I was well pleased with what we had achieved for the members. Flexible rostering brought the 39-hour working week, more free days that could be grouped together giving railwaymen longer time off work, a reduction in unsocial booking-on and -off times, and a guarantee of no compulsory redundancies.

The new rosters for the six-month experimental period had to be agreed by each local departmental committee, who had control over their operation so they could not be imposed on us by manage-ment. An extra payment was made to the guards of 50p a turn, based on the projected savings of introducing the new system of working to replace the inflexible eight-hour day.

But the sudden intransigence of the ASLEF leaders provoked the Board into refusing to pay the drivers the 3 per cent award due in January under the ACAS understanding. The ASLEF Execu-tive denounced the Board's acticn as itself being provocation. On Christmas Eve I wrote to Buckton suggesting that we meet to discuss the problem.

Further talks between the Board and ASLEF at ACAS failed to

find a solution. On 29 December I rang Buckton and asked for a meeting to establish a common strategy under the newly formed Rail Federation. I even told him I was ready to recall the NUR Executive at once although the members were on holiday. He said he would put my letter together with my request before his Executive, but I heard nothing until they decided to call a two-day national stoppage on January 13 and 14 and banned overtime working and rest-day working from the beginning of the New Year. Buckton said the crisis would worsen unless the Board honoured the backdated 3 per cent pay award agreed in August at ACAS.

ASLEF's strike decision came out of the blue. I was not given any warning by Buckton of what was going to happen. I first heard about the move on the radio and in the *Sun* newspaper. Only a week after Howell had agreed belatedly to give the go-ahead to the £30 million electrification scheme in East Anglia in direct response to the NUR deal on flexible rostering, here was a crushing setback to all our hopes for Government financial backing for British Rail's modernization plans.

Buckton kept arguing that the Board was reneging on the ACAS understanding by refusing to pay out the 3 per cent to the drivers, when the rest of the workforce received that award in January. But Parker insisted that the pay award had been dependent on agreement being reached on flexible rostering as well as the other five productivity issues. The two sides kept accusing each other of bad faith. In my opinion, they were both in the wrong.

A bit of common sense would have solved the trouble in half an hour, but instead we went on for weeks with damaging two-day stoppages by the drivers, bringing widespread havoc and misery to commuters and other rail users. The freight business was badly hit by the ASLEF 'days of action' and the Board's already hard-pressed financial position deteriorated rapidly.

ASLEF's cause found favour with the hard Left in the Labour movement. Suddenly flexible rostering – something nobody outside the railway industry had heard about before – became the major talking point in the country. The Labour Party National Executive Committee backed the ASLEF Executive, thanks to the influence of Les Huckfield, that union's representative in the House of Commons, and of Tony Benn. A further complication arose when Len Murray came out in support of Buckton's interpretation of the ACAS understandings and urged Parker to pay up the 3 per cent without waiting for a deal on flexible rostering for ASLEF drivers. Tempers rose sharply on 14 January when the Board agreed to pay the 3 per cent to the 1,600 NUR drivers who were covered by flexible rostering.

I have no doubt that hard-Left forces outside the industry were keen to stir up trouble over the issue. I was ill for a short time early in January when the crisis deepened and when I got back to the office I found the hard Left in my union were trying to inflame the guards, particularly at the London depots, into rejecting flexible rostering. Unofficial stoppages broke out, although depot after depot agreed to the introduction of the new system.

Hundreds of angry guards descended on Unity House and demanded to see me. I agreed to talk to them, though I warned that if they did not let me have a hearing I would walk out. We got together across the road from NUR headquarters at the Friends' Meeting House. I told them why we had agreed to flexible rostering for guards, and they listened to me in deadly silence. Then came the hostile questions, to loud roars of approval. But even the hard Left on my Executive had seen the sense of flexible rostering for our members, and they had voted for it when the agreement was presented to them – despite their subsequent conduct.

The Labour Shadow Cabinet was not swept along into giving support to the ASLEF cause. I went down to the Commons and made it plain to Michael Foot and other senior figures in the party that my union did not want to see Labour taking sides in the dispute by backing ASLEF. It really was a ridiculous business and made no sense at all. I could only conclude that certain people wanted to wreck the railway industry for political purposes.

Long and tedious discussions went on through January to try and resolve the crisis, but the ASLEF Executive refused to budge. They were not even prepared to co-operate with an ACAS committee of inquiry under Lord McCarthy's chairmanship. Buckton kept saying that the terms of reference should be confined to the issue of British Rail's refusal to pay the 3 per cent award and should not also cover the flexible rostering problem. Eventually McCarthy got down to work on 9 February, though without ASLEF's involvement.

I have absolutely no doubt that the sudden strikes by ASLEF in January 1982 dealt a deadly blow to the future of the railways. The goodwill that we had painfully built up with the Transport Minister was thrown away, and Howell told Parker that there was no point in having a further meeting of the Rail Council early in the year, as we had planned, to discuss more Government moves to boost investment. I decided to find out for myself what was happening, so I rang Howell and he asked me round for a private talk.

We met in a room at the House of Commons. It proved to be a depressing meeting. Howell told me that there was nothing he could do to convince his Cabinet colleagues of the case for more financial backing for the railways as long as the flexible rostering dispute had not been resolved. I pointed out that my union had delivered and there was no sense in penalizing the whole railway community because of the antics of ASLEF, but he brushed my pleas aside. It was clear to me that opinion in the Government had hardened considerably against the railway industry because of the flexible rostering nonsense.

In my submission to the ACAS committee of inquiry, I made it clear that I did not want to see any outcome to the crisis that would undermine the NUR's own agreement. In my view there was evidence enough from the discussions ASLEF had had with the Board during the autumn that its leaders had not been consistent in the intransigent line that they had taken against moving away from the eight-hour working day. I quoted what they had said at a meeting with the Board on 18 November 1981 when Buckton and his colleagues admitted they might abandon the old system if they could achieve tangible benefits from the new rostering approach.

In summing up, I told Lord McCarthy and his colleagues that there could be no shadow of doubt that the ACAS understanding committed the Board to implement fully the Tribunal decision of August 1981. This involved paying the 3 per cent to the drivers. Equally, I pointed out, we knew we were obliged to negotiate on the six areas of productivity outlined by the Board. 'While the two parties face each other in a slanging match, the industry is bleeding to death,' I told the inquiry. 'Freight is being lost, passengers are finding alternative ways of getting to work and when the dispute is over, as eventually it must be, we will be left to pick up the wreckage of the industry. Thousands of my members' jobs are threatened not only on the railways but in the workshops too. Confidence in the industry will have been seriously damaged and the real prospects of persuading Government to increase investment and to push ahead with electrification will have been sacrificed because neither party has been prepared to compromise.'

The ACAS committee of inquiry reported their decision on 16

February 1982, and Buckton hailed it as a victory for his union. The recommendations said that the Board should pay the 3 per cent backdated award and at the same time ASLEF should confirm its continued commitment to the ACAS understandings and especially flexible rostering.

Parker appeared to be in a mood to reject the committee's report and he insisted that if the issue was going to be dealt with through the existing railway conciliation machinery, then the eventual Tribunal award must be binding on everybody, including ASLEF. Without this guarantee the Board feared that the prolonged disruption by the drivers would have paid off and further prevarication would only delay a resumption of the conflict. It was only when Len Murray gave a firm assurance that the TUC's full authority would be used to secure a responsible attitude from ASLEF in negotiations and arbitration that the Board gave way.

The NUR strike

As the flexible rostering fiasco faded temporarily into the background, we faced growing trouble over our 1982 wage claim. I was seeking a substantial improvement for my members, keeping them ahead of the rate of inflation. But on 28 May the Board replied with a derisory offer of 5 per cent on basic rates from 6 September, and said that even this would not be paid out unless agreement was reached by the end of July on outstanding productivity items left over from the 1981 ACAS understandings.

I reacted angrily to this, telling the Board negotiators that the NUR had taken a positive attitude to all the efficiency items on the table. I argued that the ACAS understandings did not mean that the Board's proposals would be accepted lock, stock and barrel. The understandings included provision for negotiation, and negotiation in the NUR's book meant there would be some give on both sides.

I did not see why the entire workforce in the industry should be penalized by the Board because ASLEF would not honour any of their commitments.

Unlike them, the NUR had acted honourably in meeting its commitments on productivity, and I objected to being forced into confrontation because of somebody else's action.

The Board alleged in return that we had not responded constructively to the other efficiency items involving my members. But on the 'open station' concept, I pointed out that experiments had started in Scotland and on the Western Region, as the Board had wanted, after careful negotiation. The issue of the manning of freight trains was certainly proving more difficult to resolve, but I argued that the ACAS understanding had surely not implied the 'large-scale removal of guards'. As practical railwaymen, members of my Executive Committee expressed serious misgivings about safety if the guards were removed from non-passenger trains, but we did agree to go along with two or three experiments. However, the ASLEF dispute had delayed the planned visit to the Port Talbot-Llanwern iron-ore service in South Wales where it was to be tested out.

The 'trainman' concept was also proving tricky to resolve. The NUR was in favour of reaching agreement on this as quickly as possible because we had always wanted to see a wider range of promotional opportunities for both traffic and footplate grades and the old system had erected rigid barriers to the advance of workers. ASLEF did not approve of our approach on that issue, but the gap had been closing between us on that matter before the flexible rostering dispute began.

On the single manning of traction units, delay had been inevitable because of the deadlock over flexible rostering as the two issues were linked together.

The single biggest headache for the NUR was the manning of the new Bedford-London St Pancras electrified service which was due to start in May 1982. The Board wanted to make the service a one-man operation and they told us this in May 1981, though they knew the union was totally opposed to the idea. On 11 June, a few weeks after being told of the Board's intentions, I wrote back and confirmed that 'under no circumstances' was I able to discuss one-man operation of trains. The ACAS understanding had spoken of looking at the issue without 'any preconceived conditions on either side', but it had also been clear from our prolonged talks with the Board that the problem was linked to the open station. If staff were to be withdrawn from the selling and taking of tickets, then this would provide a new role for guards on the electrified service. Bedford-London St Pancras was seen as the prototype for the whole South-East commuter rail area. The Board had spent £150 million on new signalling and rolling stock for the service without even consulting us. Yet despite this I was ready at our meeting on 15 February 1982 to make a compromise. Our proposals involved giving the guards a new role in protecting revenue on the trains which would be applied for a trial period, while all workers operating the new system would have a new pay and grading structure. I took the view that the Board was taking too narrow a view of the problem and they should look at the Bedford-St Pancras line as an entity, for with a considerable drop in the number of signalmen and other grades there had already been a substantial fall in the total numbers employed on the service.

It was not just the differences between us on the outstanding efficiency issues that worsened relations between my union and the Board in late May and early June of 1982. Periodically I and my colleagues used to go for lunch with Parker and other Board members to discuss the state of the railway industry. Over a meal at Rail House in early May I was suddenly told that the Board had decided to close the Shildon rail works in County Durham with the loss of 2,450 jobs and to run down both the works at Horwich near Bolton with a further 1,650 jobs to go and at Swindon with 1,500 more redundancies.

I could hardly believe my ears. 'Say that again,' I told Parker. 'Do you think I'm going to Shildon and telling them they're finished?' I warned him: 'You have plenty enough on your plate without taking this on. You close those workshops over my dead body.' The Board insisted they simply had not got enough orders for building, maintenance and repair to justify keeping all the twelve BREL engineering works operating. The cutbacks in locomotive fleets had lessened the workload, and Shildon's order books were empty.

But their plans would have had grave consequences. Shildon depot was vital to the small town in County Durham, because there is simply no other work available there, and the town was already suffering high unemployment.

Parker and his Board members ignored my views and notified me officially a few days later of their intentions. In the subsequent discussion with my Executive Committee on both the workshop situation and the pay offer, I recommended that unless the Board withdrew their proposals over Shildon, Horwich and Swindon and also made a better pay offer by 7 June, we would instruct our members to take industrial action.

I had in mind using a form of disruption which would cause the maximum damage and produce a quick result, using key groups like the signalmen, so as to avoid a drawn-out dispute. I presented an option paper to the Executive of possible strategies, but the selective aproach was the one I thought the most sensible.

I was due to attend the conference of the Canadian Trades Union Congress in Winnipeg as a TUC representative along with Sir John Boyd of the AUEW. Russell Tuck and Charlie Turnock were left with the task of persuading the Executive to adopt my preferred course of industrial action, but unfortunately they failed to make any impression on the Executive Committee members who were determined to call everybody out on strike. When I arrived at Heathrow airport on 4 June after my Canadian trip, I was handed a letter from the Board. This announced a reprieve for Shildon, Horwich and Swindon.

But if the Board were ready to back down on the engineering workshops, they showed no similar flexibility over their basic 5 per cent pay offer linked to a breakthrough on productivity. My Executive Committee rejected my plan for selective action and decided to call an all-out strike of the entire membership from midnight on June 27/28 unless the Board improved its offer. I had been forced up against the buffers by the Board, and I saw our hopes of Government backing for modernization receding even farther.

Some people believe wrongly that the setting of the strike date for 28 June was chosen deliberately by me to sabotage the conflict. On that day the NUR annual conference was gathering in Plymouth. For the length of the conference the power of decision-making rests with the 77 delegates and not the Executive Committee, which is dissolved for the interim. However, it was not by design but by sheer logic that the strike was set for 28 June, for a good fortnight was needed to finalize our preparations. Indeed, a move was made unsuccessfully to start the dispute on 30 June, three days into the conference. But I am sure that the hard Left on the Executive Committee believed that the delegates would be swept along by the sheer momentum of events into rubber-stamping their strike decision.

Later, I was accused of not giving my whole-hearted support to mobilizing the members for the strike, but again this is untrue. We pulled out all the stops at Head Office to organize for the stoppage. I insisted that the Executive members must attend special meetings of the twenty-six district councils which I had arranged to find out the mood of the rank and file. Reports were sent back to me in Euston Road, but the hard-Left Executive members did not convey an accurate picture of membership feelings. Indeed, I could see signs of growing opposition among the rank and file to the all-out strike call. Messages and telegrams reaching my office expressed criticism or doubt.

I soon realized that the majority of delegates at our annual conference would not back the strike action. They were far less dominated by hard-Left ideology and much more in touch with grassroots opinion than the Executive Committee.

The strike started as planned at midnight on 28 June. It was the first total shutdown of the railway industry since 1955. I told a press conference in Plymouth on the eve of our own conference that I would be in touch with ACAS Chairman Pat Lowry to see if negotiations could be reopened.

In my speech to the delegates on Monday morning I was very careful to avoid strengthening hard-Left accusations that I was being less than whole-hearted in supporting the strike, but I made it abundantly clear to the delegates that it was up to them alone to decide whether the disruption should continue or not. I did not have to make an emotional speech one way or the other. There was no need for me to launch into any arguments to persuade the majority of delegates to follow a certain course of action.

A delegate moved a motion which proposed placing the whole pay issue with the McCarthy Tribunal and calling the strike off. He was convinced that the NUR had such a good case that the Tribunal, after considering all the evidence, would make a favourable award. After a lengthy debate the delegates voted by a convincing 47 to 30 to adopt that resolution.

The end of the rail strike after only two days was no defeat for my members. It accurately reflected the views of the vast majority, who disliked the pay offer being made to them by the Board, but saw no sense at all in bringing the whole industry to a standstill without first testing our claim before McCarthy.

I was increasingly aware that industrial disruption on the railways was now counter-productive. During the ASLEF flexible rostering stoppages in January and February 1982 the road hauliers and the coach operators made a killing at our expense. Britain could survive quite well for some time without us if it needed to. Our ultimate threat of being able to paralyse the economy through the use of our industrial muscle was becoming a thing of the past. The irresponsible strike tactics of ASLEF had begun to expose our weakness, and we were therefore playing into the hands of our enemies. In taking our case to the McCarthy Tribunal we were following the only sensible course of action left open to us. But we had come very close to disaster before making that decision, and my hard-Left dominated Executive Committee would certainly not have made it left to its own devices.

ASLEF strikes again

As our stoppage came to an early end, suddenly the ASLEF Executive decided on an indefinite all-out strike by drivers from 4 July. The reason was again flexible rostering.

This festering issue had come to a head again after the McCarthy Tribunal had reached its decision on 7 May. Its report said that ASLEF should accept the new system, which introduced shifts varying between seven and nine hours and ended the former guaranteed eight-hour day. The rosters were to be negotiated at each depot, and if there were any differences of opinion these would be resolved inside the conciliation machinery of the industry. Every difficulty raised by ASLEF at the Tribunal was met with specific safeguards written into the award, so that the drivers would have their worries dealt with.

But Buckton rejected the McCarthy award out of hand as 'totally unacceptable'. His Executive followed suit. On 28 May the Board tried again to get the ASLEF leaders to see some sense by urging them to reconsider their position and make an effort to negotiate an agreement. To prepare for the new system the Board proposed to start issuing the rosters at depot level. Jim Urquhart, the Board member responsible for improved productivity plans, said the Board intended to impose the rosters if necessary on the drivers if ASLEF's leaders refused to see sense.

The British Rail Board bent over backwards to try and please ASLEF. At a meeting on 17 June ASLEF leaders did seem to be modifying their hardline position when they suggested that they were always ready to examine the flexible rostering question, though they remained convinced that this could be achieved through existing agreements. For its part, the Board suggested an experiment on its flexible rostering proposals in one area such as Scotland, while ASLEF could try out its own alternative method in another part of the network.

The Board repeated their offer on 22 June. Later in that meeting Buckton said they might agree to trials in two places if it meant no imposition of rosters anywhere in the meantime, and on the understanding that the ASLEF delegate conference could turn it down at a special meeting.

Buckton was to report back to his Executive on 28 June on the experiment and tell Parker the outcome as soon as he could. British Rail reinforced this suggestion by planning to impose flexible rosters on drivers at the depots from 5 July unless ASLEF gave a commitment on the two experiments. In a letter to Buckton on 25 June the Board confirmed that the experiments would start on 31 July for three months, and in return the instructions to managers to implement the new rosters from 4 July would be withdrawn.

I think the Board was being far too lenient with ASLEF, after all that we had been through, and perhaps Buckton and his Executive thought the Board was on the run because it had offered a compromise so late in the day, suggesting that it would not stand firm on the flexible rostering issue. Indeed, I believe that Parker and his colleagues were far too soft in dealing with the drivers' union during my whole time as NUR General Secretary.

Anyway, on 28 June the Board sent Buckton a further letter that confirmed the two experiments and the withdrawal of the instructions for imposing the rosters. The next day the Board rang up Arkwright Road to find out whether the ASLEF Executive had yet discussed the proposals, and was told that it had not. At this point Buckton was reminded that unless the Board received a satisfactory reply to the proposal by the evening of 30 June, then the rosters would be imposed on 5 July.

I believe ASLEF thought we would be having a confrontation with the Board on the pay issue, so they were taken aback when our dispute proved to be short-lived. At no stage did Buckton or anybody else in Arkwright Road bother to contact me in Plymouth and tell me what was going on.

Instead, only hours before my members were due to return to work after their two days' strike, the ASLEF Executive announced an all-out strike in protest at British Rail's planned imposition of flexible rosters at the depots. The World Cup was being played at the time and one arrogant ASLEF spokesman compared his union and mine when he blustered to British Rail: 'You are not playing Kuwait now, you are playing Brazil.' My reply was: 'If I was a Brazilian footballer and I was compared to that crowd, I would burn my bloody boots tomorrow.'

I placed the ASLEF strike decision before the Plymouth conference to decide our course for action. Delegates were shocked and angered by the antics of the drivers' union, which had told its members to work normally during our dispute and to cross our picket lines. 'How many times do you have to turn the other cheek? How many times do you have to be meek and mild, humble and forgiving?' I asked. I accused ASLEF of 'tearing up agreements like confetti', and its Executive of being 'misguided, stupid and inconsiderate'. We told our drivers not to cross ASLEF picket lines but instructed the rest of the members to report for work as usual. As time goes by I am more than ever convinced that outside, hard-Left political influences were focused in the summer of 1982 to provoke a confrontation on the railways by one means or another, as I will discuss later. They had tried their best to drive the NUR into a strike and they failed. Now the ASLEF Executive provided the opportunity for a showdown with the Board, and above all with the Tory Government.

But Mrs Thatcher, still basking in the reflected glory of the Falklands victory, was in no mood to bow the knee to Ray Buckton and his Executive. She made a ferocious speech on Cheltenham racecourse against the drivers, calling on the so-called 'Falklands spirit' to crush them.

The ASLEF strike began as planned on 4 July, but it was clear from the start that the loyalty of the train drivers was being stretched to the limit. In many regions there were signs of a rank-and-file revolt and some trains were running. But then Michael Foot stepped into the crisis. He was due to speak on 10 July at the Durham miners' gala. In the written version of his speech, which had obviously been drafted by someone without the slightest understanding of the arguments, he threw his support behind ASLEF in their dispute, suggesting that the Board showed 'an extraordinary desire to pick a fight with the rail unions'. This document, circulated to the press, claimed that ASLEF had 'offered a sensible way out of the problem. But the Board – with the Government pushing them – were adamant that they would have a strike and they got one.' The Shadow Transport Minister, Albert Booth, again apparently ignorant of the real issues, also jointed in support for the ASLEF Executive.

This stupid intervention merely encouraged Buckton and his colleagues to carry on with their suicidal behaviour. In fact, Foot did not deliver that part of his speech in Durham, but it had already been released to journalists in London so the fat was in the fire. Next day I had to tell the press: 'He wants to be careful what he says. No amount of smokescreens can hide the fact that the train drivers have refused to accept a decision on flexible rostering which my union is operating.'

I went and saw Foot privately at the House of Commons, together with the NUR MPs and senior Shadow Cabinet members. It was a rather rough meeting, as I was pretty outspoken. I was concerned at the Labour Party leader, who obviously did not know all the facts having exposed himself in this way, a situation which the Tory party would exploit to the maximum – and they did. Mrs Thatcher called Foot 'the striker's friend'.

As the all-out drivers' dispute entered its second week Parker and the Board decided to get tough. They threatened to sack all 23,000 ASLEF members and close down the network within seven days unless the drivers returned to work and accepted flexible rostering in principle. On hearing this I said: 'We are now at the crossroads. The future of British Rail will be decided this week. Thousands of jobs and thousands of miles of railway track will go down the plughole. The train drivers will go down the plughole like everybody else. The sooner the strike is called off the better.'

Personally I did not welcome the ultimatum from the Board. I thought it was needlessly provocative and might even harden attitudes among the striking drivers. But now the TUC intervened because of the mounting pressure on Congress House from other unions. An emergency meeting of the TUC's 'inner cabinet' – the Finance and General Purposes Committee – was called together for 16 July to work out a settlement to end the conflict.

All the rail union leaders were called in. I was jostled and shouted at by the 'rent-a-mob' outside the TUC headquarters and I needed police protection. In contrast, Buckton arrived to a hero's welcome. Left-wingers such as Allan Sapper, the TUC's Chairman for the year and General Secretary of the Association of Cinematography, Television and Allied Technicians (ACTT) vowed his undying support for ASLEF on his way into the meeting. He had been backing the ASLEF case on public platforms.

But inside Congress House the mood was quite different and much more realistic. We sat in separate rooms, ACAS style, while the TUC Finance and General Purposes Committee tried to solve the crisis. It took Len Murray and his colleagues less than an hour and a half to decide that the ASLEF case was non-existent. The drivers' union had to bite the bullet whether they liked it or not. Nevertheless, it had taken Len Murray until very late in the day to see the harsh facts staring us all in the face.

At a press conference in February 1982, explaining the flexible rostering dispute

Right The earliest photograph of me, taken at the age of ten
Below My family outside Buckingham Palace when my father was awarded the MBE in 1966. From left to right: my sister Brenda, father, mother, my brother Maurice and my sister Elma
Opposite At home with my father in 1971, after a presentation to him by the local NUR branch

JAPAN

U.S.A.

INTERPRETER

GREAT BRITAIN

Above   Selected for a conference of
the International Transport Workers
Federation as delegate for the
Railwaymen's section in Utrecht,
1951. With me are our president,
Harry Franklin (in the bow tie), and
members of the Executive
Right   A young hopeful – taken in
1948 when I was agent for the
Richmond Constituency Labour
Party
Opposite   My footballing days

Left   The press were already outside Number 10 for my 'unofficial' visit to Harold Wilson to avoid a national shutdown in 1975
Above   Ray Buckton and I taking time off from an International Transport Workers Federation Conference at Harrogate in 1976

Above   The 1975 Executive of the NUR, in the boardroom of the old Unity House. To my left is the president, David Bowman, and standing is Frank Cannon, the Assistant General Secretary

Above right   I have always believed in buying my own ticket – as my grandfather said, nothing from the bosses!

Right   It is only by constant contact with the rank and file that you can really represent the membership. Birmingham, 1978

Left   Jim Callaghan and I at the opening of our Educational Centre at Frant in April 1977
Top   Lord of the Manor, Frant
Above   Back on the footplate, at Shildon in 1975 to celebrate 150 years of railways

Right Laying down the law to Arthur Scargill! On a visit to Kellingley pit in December 1980
Below Forging international links is an important role for a modern union. At the 1980 congress of the International Transport Workers Federation in Florida

Left Relief at the calling-off
of a national strike in August
1981. Tom Jenkins of the
TSSA is to my right and Ray
Buckton of ASLEF to my left
Below The Triple Alliance:
with Joe Gormley of the
NUM (in the middle) and Bill
Sirs of the ISTC at the
Alliance's formation

Above left   With a police escort going into the NUR conference at Birmingham
in October 1982
Left   Leaving Unity House by the back door after my resignation, in a fruitless
attempt to avoid the press
Above   The Special Labour Party conference at Wembley in 1981. Lined up
behind me (in the front row from left to right) Frank Allaun, Tony Benn, Alec
Kitson, Ron Hayward and Norman Atkinson, with Dennis Skinner behind
Frank Allaun

Packing up in my office, just before Christmas 1982

ASLEF had effectively isolated itself in the trade union movement through its own folly. TUC leaders were to spend nearly twenty-four hours of intensive, non-stop discussion at Congress House and with ACAS to find some face-saving formula to help Buckton and his stubborn Executive off the hook on which they had impaled themselves.

Finally at breakfast time on Saturday morning Murray and Sapper told ASLEF's Executive that the strike must be called off and they had to accept flexible rostering in principle. The annual conference of ASLEF should be brought back within a week to ten days to agree and rosters should be worked in the seventy-one depots where they had already been imposed. The only concession ASLEF received was an assurance that no more rosters would be imposed until negotiations were completed.

The ASLEF Executive went back to Arkwright Road and spent most of the weekend deciding what to do. Eventually a defeated Buckton announced to the press on Sunday 18 July that they had agreed to accept the TUC-imposed terms. He had some harsh words to say about me, accusing me of having 'assisted British Railways Board at every stage' and of making public utterances that were 'contrary to every principle of trade unionism'.

I replied quickly that if I had been attacked by Buckton for honouring our commitments and agreements I belonged to a different sort of trade union movement from his. I also said that I was delighted that the strike was over.

The hard Left squealed afterwards that ASLEF had been betrayed by the TUC. It was even reported that moderate members of the Finance and General Purposes Committee such as Frank Chapple, Terry Duffy and Tom Jackson had outvoted the broad-Left leaders to impose a settlement on Buckton and his Executive.

There was not a shred of truth in that accusation. No doubt, some Left-wingers wanted to improve their credentials with ASLEF, who were seen by some as a Praetorian guard among the hard Left in the trade union movement. But Sapper, who had previously spoken in support of them, Moss Evans of the TGWU and Clive Jenkins of the Association of Scientific, Technical and Managerial Staffs (ASTMS) all saw that ASLEF could not carry on any longer. The facts spoke for themselves and nobody could deny that Buckton and his Executive were in an impossible position.

In fact, I believe that the TUC saved ASLEF from self-destruction and its own leaders knew this perfectly well though they would not admit it. A mass return to work among demoralized train drivers was only days away at the end. The collapse of the dispute would certainly have happened quickly if the TUC had not moved in and forced ASLEF to call it off.

ASLEF played into the hands of the enemies of the railways. Their 1982 strikes were disastrous to the system's interests. They were mounted on the wrong issue and staged at the wrong time and for the wrong reason. The flexible rostering disputes lost us vital support in the Cabinet, where Mrs Thatcher and more unsympathetic Ministers had their prejudices against the industry confirmed by the stoppages, and she subsequently sacked David Howell. The Government set up yet another committee of inquiry to look at British Rail's finances, under Sir David Serpell, a Board member and former civil servant. In January 1983 it produced its report, which was utterly negative and spelt out a grim future for the railways, completely rejecting Parker's hopes for an improved network.

Modernizing the Union

Changing the Executive

I came to power in the NUR with a clear determination to bring the union into the last quarter of the twentieth century. As Assistant General Secretary, I had come round increasingly to the view that the union needed thoroughgoing reform to make it a much more effective organization.

As the first industrial trade union in Britain the NUR, with its constitution drawn up in 1913, has in most respects stood the test of time. Its founding fathers were far-sighted in trying to marry effective worker democracy in the union with an efficient administration, but they could not have expected to plan for the massive changes that have taken place in the structure of transport over the past seventy years and the masses of legislation affecting transport and industrial relations.

In the post-war period many members recognized that changes in the NUR's structure were necessary, but it is never easy to reform trade union organizations. The pressures for doing nothing can be intense, and any change can stir up a hornet's nest. Attempts were made in the 1950s to overhaul the structure, but they foundered. A further effort was made in the 1960s, but the annual conference could not agree on a formula.

The most important reform we needed to make was to ensure that our National Executive Committee was much more representative of the wide range of members we had inside the union. The composition had not been changed in sixty years. Twenty-four members were elected through six geographical areas of the union

99

whose boundaries had remained almost the same. Each district elected a representative from each of four sections. These were classed as Locomotive; Traffic; Goods and Cartage; and Workshops and the Permanent Way.

The trouble was that the system ensured that some groups of members were better represented than others. The Locomotive section had only 3,000 members and yet it had six seats on the Executive Committee, while the Traffic section boasted over 82,800 members and Workshops and Permanent Way nearly 67,000 members, but each only had the same six seats on the Committee.

Moreover, those bigger sections covered a wide range of different jobs. Traffic included managers, signalmen, cleaners and people who were employed in British Transport Hotels, while the 17,900 members of Goods and Cartage came from National Carriers, Freightliners, British Rail Shipping and the British Transport Docks Board among other organizations.

As a result of this, Executive members, who were elected from each group for periods of three years before going back to their old jobs, had to assume responsibility for matters that affected grades and railway work that fell outside their own direct experience. The inevitable tendency was for the larger membership groups to dominate the Executive elections.

In Goods and Cartage, for example, National Carriers were over-represented when compared with members in dock and shipping. The big railway workshops were far more likely to have representatives on the Executive than permanent way staff. Guards and signalmen were historically over-represented on the Executive, whereas hotel staff and station workers were rarely seen there.

This concern with the structure of the Executive Committee of the union is important because in the NUR the Executive Committee has a much bigger role to play than similar bodies in other unions. Its full-time members take an active part in all the wage negotiations we carry out. They supervise and control the flow of work going through Head Office on negotiations and they take decisions at every stage of our machinery on how a particular case should be handled.

We have fewer full-time officers in the union where branches come together for consultative and propaganda purposes, but a big gulf exists between the depots and stations and Head Office.

After the failures of the two previous decades the 1977 conference agreed with me that we should appoint some independent outside industrial relations experts to advise us on how to change the Executive Committee structure. I approached Warwick University's industrial relations research unit and it agreed to take on the job. The Warwick team presented its final report to the 1978 annual conference. This proposed that we should keep the existing six geographical areas for the Executive representation, but increase the number of departmental groupings from four to five. The proposed new groups would cover traffic and locomotive; permanent way; workshops; road transport and London Transport; and docks and hotels. As well as the proposed changes on the Executive Committee, the report called for the national grade and group conferences in the union to be included in the rulebook with clearly defined functions.

An effort was made by the hard Left on the Executive to stop any changes on the lines suggested by Warwick, but it failed and at the 1978 annual conference delegates voted by 65 votes to 15 to accept the recommendations for the Executive. It was more difficult to win approval for the other proposed reform. This involved the grade and group conferences created to deal with the specific problems of special categories like signalmen and guards. However, after a lengthy discussion inside the union, the July 1979 annual conference voted narrowly by 40 votes to 37 to accept that change as well. Eleven grade conferences were recognized as a result.

These changes might seem limited and unimportant, but they reveal how difficult it can be for any union to reform itself. I found the whole business exhausting, but I was glad that we had broken the impasse. Later, though, growing trouble with the Executive Committee made me realize that we had not gone far enough in the reform process.

Training the members
I was anxious to give top priority to the education of our members. The general level of training facilities is totally inadequate in most unions, so I wanted the NUR to come to the front in this vital area. Without adequate training for its activities a trade union today finds it very difficult to function efficiently. Our union had a good reputation for education, particularly through its involvement with the National Labour College, but by the early 1970s district

101

council weekend schools and TUC postal courses and residential schools were not enough to meet the needs of a modern union.

Shortly after taking over as General Secretary, I came across an ideal property for an educational centre for the union, a large residential house at Frant near Tunbridge Wells in Kent, with forty-four acres of beautiful grounds. I had to act quickly to get it. Going through the Executive Committee would have been far too slow and the union might have lost the property as a result. I therefore used the union's holding company to make the purchase and presented the idea of establishing a national education centre to the Executive after all the buying problems had been dealt with.

It made sense to sell off thirty acres of land around the grounds immediately adjacent to the house, so I suggested that we do this to my Executive Committee. To my surprise, they raised no objections to the purchase of Frant Place and its conversion into an education centre, but they did oppose the idea of selling off the land. I decided the best step to take was to take them all down to the property so they could see it for themselves. I hired a coach for the day and we all went to Frant.

The land agent spent the whole morning trying to explain that what he had in mind was in the best interests of the union but the Executive members would have none of it, insisting that the union should hold on to the 30 acres as an investment. At lunchtime I invited the land agent to join us all in a nearby pub for a pint and a sandwich, but he said he had had enough for one day. 'No wonder you have problems with your Executive,' he told me. The union is now looking after the whole estate with a couple of gardeners and the help of a local farmer. The NUR has become the lord of the manor, to the amusement of the popular press!

Frant Educational Centre was officially opened by Jim Callaghan, then Prime Minister, on 30 April 1977. With the able assistance of Frank Cannon, my Assistant General Secretary, and considerable help from district officers Bill Robinson and Brian Arundel, and later Ben Stoneham who came from the National Coal Board to take on the task of educational officer, we developed the union's educational services quickly. Over 800 students a year are now passing through Frant Place on courses and the Centre is open throughout the year. We have some of the best facilities for trade union education in the movement.

I also developed joint trade union-management courses, because it was vital in my opinion to make sure we knew each other's problems if we hoped to make a success of a public sector industry like the railways. I even extended this to joint management-national executive discussions at Frant Place and also in our Boardroom, but these sessions had to be stopped eventually in later years because of the Left-wing attitudes of a growing number of Executive members, which made such meetings with British Rail management impossible. Some of the hard Left told me these were just exercises in brainwashing from people who were the enemies of the working class. Similar attitudes were demonstrated at the 1983 conference towards the BR Chairman.

I also had increasing trouble from them over Ben Stoneham, the union's education officer. He had been Labour candidate for Saffron Walden in the 1979 general election, but he joined the Social Democratic Party when it was formed. As a result, he came under constant pressure inside the union to give up his job. Extreme elements on the Executive Committee were always demanding that I should sack him.

I refused point blank to take action against a man on political grounds. We had not prevented Communists from working in the office or serving on the Executive Committee. We did not ban Left-wing extremists such as the Militant Tendency, who were becoming more and more prominent in the union. However, some people in the office sent Stoneham to Coventry and refused to speak to him. He finally left to start educational activities at Sainsbury's and the union lost a first-class education officer. Such is the intolerance of the extreme Left.

A new Unity House

Unity House, our headquarters in London on the Euston Road, had been the home of railway trade unionism since 1910. It symbolized the arrival of the railway workers as an industrial and political force in the country. The marble corridors resembled the inside of a Victorian Gothic town hall, recalling the great days of the age of steam. Unity House had seen many memorable events in our history. A year after it opened came the 1911 railway strike, the first national shutdown of the industry, and our headquarters was the centre of operations around the clock.

On 29 March 1913 the NUR was inaugurated, in succession to the Amalgamated Society of Railway Servants. It was the first serious attempt to organize an industrial union. Unity House became a source of inspiration for hundreds of thousands of trade unionists. Between the World Wars, in 1919, in 1921 and again in 1926 during the General Strike, Unity House provided the focus for our solidarity.

The offices were steeped in Labour history, but it was difficult to run a modern union with the facilities available in the old building. The working conditions for the administrative staff were shocking and the office manager was constantly drawing my attention to the many repairs that needed doing.

Here was an occasion when the hard economic facts of life dictated that we should cast sentiment aside. One day in 1975, soon after I became General Secretary, a group of developers acting on behalf of our neighbours the Wellcome Institute asked to see me. They said they wanted to buy Unity House, redevelop the site and provide enough space for the NUR to stay at a peppercorn rent on a 99-year lease. It was a tempting proposition. However, I began to think it might be more sensible if we rebuilt the headquarters ourselves and paid for it. I struggled for quite a while with the problem of whether to knock down Unity House. The generation of my grandfather and father had looked to our headquarters as a symbol of what the union stood for. The decision to go ahead came only after hours of agonizing. What finally made up my mind was a discussion I had with Sir John Benstead, a former union General Secretary, at a meeting over tea at the Station Hotel in Peterborough. I told him what I was considering and asked him what he would do in my position.

Without batting an eyelid, he said you could not live on memories of the past, but you had to look to the future. If Unity House had served its purpose, it should be knocked down; but, he said, make sure you build the new office well so that it would be a credit to the NUR.

I started to find out whether it could be done. First of all an office development permit was needed. I made contact with the Department of the Environment, where Tony Crosland was most helpful. Representatives from the Department looked over Unity House and they agreed it was unreasonable for the staff to continue working in such conditions.

The permit was granted. The next stage was to get authority from Camden Borough Council. They sent their planning committee along, who agreed to what we wanted to do. We began to make inquiries into the problems we would have to face. Armed with these facts, I presented the proposal for a new building to the

Executive Committee, who finally gave me the authority to proceed.

But in the meantime local elections in Camden had led to a change on the planning committee, which now reconsidered the original decisions about Unity House. We had already spent a great deal of money based on the first go-ahead, and I was very angry at the council's attitude to a long-standing member of the Camden community and a substantial ratepayer. This prevarication delayed the project needlessly, but they eventually agreed we could proceed.

The next problem was to find a temporary, alternative office while Unity House was being rebuilt. Cambridge University Press had a building just across the road from us and they offered accommodation for rent, but I persuaded my Executive Committee to buy up the property for £2.36 million because it was bound to appreciate in value. There were obvious advantages in moving such a short distance. When we were ready to occupy the new Unity House, we sold off the property for £3.5 million to our next-door neighbours the Wellcome Institute, who had first put the idea into my head. They now have extra property near their own Head Office, and we have a new building worthy of the union and fit for its future.

Not only do the new premises provide modern air-conditioned accommodation for the union's employees, they also provide over 23,000 square feet net of space to be let. This extra accommodation is completely self-contained and occupies a prime site in London, being near Euston and three underground stations.

The new Unity House has six floors and includes a large conference room. Various items of interest have been kept from the old building and incorporated in the new, including the oval glass dome, panelling in the boardroom and numerous stained-glass panels. In the reception hall there is a large illuminated stained-glass screen depicting the union's history and progress over the years from 1872 to the present day.

The new building was officially opened on 3 May 1983. The Executive Committee, as a deliberate slight, did not invite me to the ceremony, but you cannot afford to waste your time worrying about the decisions of intellectual pygmies. I rest content that I achieved my objective of creating a Head Office for the NUR which will ensure it becomes one of the best equipped unions in Britain. My father and grandfather would have been proud of it.

Updating the union

During my time as General Secretary, I also made many important changes in our administration at Head Office. Thirty years ago a union like the NUR was still able to recruit all the staff it needed from among its own members, but this is no longer the case. I was forced to widen our recruitment area so that we could have employees with the necessary special skills to service the many needs of the union.

We took on a growing number of university graduates and others who did not necessarily have any family background in the railway industry. On balance this was a successful policy. Our research papers and the back-up material busy trade union officers require improved in quality. But as the raucous hard Left on the Executive Committee grew more troublesome, I began to have serious doubts about the loyalties of some people in the office.

I created a special research department in the union to cope with our wide range of problems. This caused few difficulties except the unusual one of headquarters staff who resented specialists being recruited to work in the new department. I have always found it difficult to understand this attitude when clearly it was in the interests of the union and its members to employ the best possible people with high qualifications.

I also launched an effort to improve our communications and publicity with our members and the world outside the union. Our weekly newspaper had its name changed from the *Railway* to the *Transport Review*. The reason for this was obvious enough. The changing nature of transport in Britain involved the NUR, and everybody needed to know what was going on.

When I took over the circulation of the paper was only about 7,000 and it was sold to the members through the branches and at some newsagents. I believed it was much more sensible to give the paper away and make it fortnightly, so that it could deal in more depth with important political and industrial issues. The re-vamped *Review* stimulated much more response.

I backed up the *Review* with regular newsletters directed to each undertaking in the industry, such as London Transport and British Rail Engineering. I was convinced that it was only by giving much more attention to the widest possible circulation of material that we could tackle the widespread apathy and stimulate interest among the members towards attending union branch meetings and local Labour parties.

I was becoming increasingly aware that this apathy would end up creating tremendous problems for the union. It would either die because of the lack of interest among the rank and file or it would be taken over by extreme political elements who were totally unrepresentative of the membership. It is certainly true that branch and district council attendances in the NUR went down dramatically in the late sixties and seventies.

But even my modest changes in the union newspaper brought opposition from some Left-wing members of the union, who claimed quite wrongly that it had been turned into a mouthpiece of the General Secretary.

Another initiative I took to widen interest in our affairs was to let the press give a greater coverage to the annual conference. When I took over as General Secretary the practice was that they were allowed to listen to only two or three specific debates. On that basis very few newspapers were ready to send their industrial correspondents to cover our conferences, which was hardly surprising. From 1975 on we threw open the whole first week of our fortnight of deliberations to the press, and nobody could doubt that the publicity we had as a result kept the NUR in the public eye, for good or ill.

All the changes I made to modernize the union involved long hours of debate which became exhausting at times. But they were all of such vital importance to the future of the union that they had to be given a high priority, despite the fact that we had many other pressing problems.

Fortunately I had a number of good colleagues in Head Office on whom I could rely to share the burdens. Without their help I would never have got through the changes. In fact, looking back I am amazed at just how much we did in reforming the union, in the face of determined opposition from many people on the Executive Committee.

A further area for reform which I had in mind, but never got round to doing anything about, was the election to national office of the Executive Committee and full-time officials. The NUR electoral system is open to abuse. Indeed, I believe it needs only half a dozen dedicated people to take over any branch in the union. There are some branches that do not even meet at all.

The block vote system of voting in the NUR does not really stand serious examination, because the votes of all the members of the branch whether they turn up or not are cast for one individual candidate. This means, for example, that an NUR branch might have 300 members of whom only ten might go to the meeting where the election is held, and of that number six might vote for one candidate and four for another, but all 300 votes would go to the winner in the contest.

One sensible way forward would be to introduce secret ballot voting for the Executive Committee and full-time officials on the job at the point of employment in the depots, stations and works. If the members work in scattered areas, it might be sensible to have voting where they collect their wage packets. There should be an individual vote for all the national positions in the union.

I have no time for Norman Tebbit's plans for trade union democracy because I believe unions should reform themselves and not have laws imposed upon them to make them change their ways. Nevertheless, if we don't put our own house in order ourselves to combat the apathy in the branches, we are asking for Government intervention.

I also believe that if we are going to expect loyalty from the membership in national strike decisions, the rank and file must be consulted. In the dispute of June 1982, for example, many members of the Executive Committee did not give an accurate picture of the genuine mood among their members in the branches and district councils who did not want to strike.

Why the closed shop?
Trade union democracy is essential to a just operation of the closed shop. If we find members rebelling because they feel that their views are not taken fully into account, and we then retaliate by withdrawing their union membership cards or depriving them of union benefits, we will certainly build up the pressures from our political opponents to abolish the closed shop agreement, and rightly. Nevertheless, the closed shop is still necessary to a disciplined trade union workforce.

My support for it shocks many people, who argue that it is a tyrannical device to crush the freedom of individual workers. This point of view misunderstands the purposes of trade unionism.

The closed shop agreements that my union signed with British Rail and other organizations such as the hotels were in the best interests of management, unions and the workforce. In 1969 compulsory trade union membership was introduced on the railways. It became a condition of employment for all staff in the industry after 1 January 1970 that they should belong to a union which was recognized in the machinery for negotiation on the railways.

The closed shop was part of a much wider pay and efficiency package negotiated at that time, but it was the culmination of a long campaign by my union dating from the 1930s. That agreement lasted only two years, for the Tories overthrew it by their 1971 Industrial Relations Act. But when that controversial measure was repealed by the Labour Government in 1974, I negotiated a much stricter closed shop agreement that made no exceptions for workers who did not want to join the appropriate union unless they could provide evidence of 'genuine religious belief' that made it impossible for them to belong to a union. This caused few problems, and later in 1975 the system was extended to British Rail hotel staff. I achieved this by refusing to sign a very important agreement with the Board unless it accepted that the closed shop should cover the hotel staff as well as the railwaymen. Despite the initial hostility of the hotel management to this move, they eventually recognized the obligations that such an agreement imposed on us and they appreciated the value of good labour relations which came from the closed shop.

Later on when the hotels were sold off under Tory privatization plans, we were able to persuade the new company running the Gleneagles Hotel in Scotland and their investors of the merits of the closed shop agreement to them. It became one of the conditions of the sale of Gleneagles in 1981 that the 100 per cent union arrangement should stay. This also applied to subsequent sales of British Transport hotels.

Quite honestly, the people who don't want to join a union that negotiates at their workplace are a running sore in our midst. Nine-tenths of them are the worst sort of employee, the sort who take everything and give nothing. They are an aggravation and I have no time for them. My attitude to the closed shop is not authoritarian. I have been to many countries behind the Iron Curtain and I certainly would not like to live in any of those places. I am a nonconformist at heart. I don't click my heels and I resent anybody who says people should.

It is the history of our union and the memories of what happened to my father and grandfather that determine my outlook to the closed shop. They told me of how men were victimized and kicked out of their homes by the railway company because they wanted to belong to a trade union. It took us thirty-nine years of struggle on the railways to achieve recognition of the NUR by the employers. Little wonder that my father's and grandfather's generation felt utter contempt for those men who sat on the sidelines without joining the union.

It is only reasonable that workers feel it is unfair and get angry when they see people unwilling to join a union at work, but who are very willing to accept wage rises, shorter hours and longer holidays won by the union for all the workers. Moreover, the closed shop agreement we negotiated brought British Rail positive advantages because we for our part pledged to observe procedures and clamp down on unofficial disruption if it broke out anywhere. If I had said I wanted to tear up the closed shop agreement, the Board members would have gone white in the face.

Nobody can contract out of the rules of modern society. Otherwise the whole thing would become chaos. In return for that order some individual freedom is inevitably lost. If you say you're free not to join a union, others are equally free to say they won't work with you. If you just want to be an awkward customer and not a member of the human race, you had better find yourself another planet. I believe in liberty but I don't believe in licence. Nobody should do as they like irrespective of how it affects their fellow men.

There was only one occasion when we were tested to the hilt on accepting our obligations under the closed shop agreement. In August 1978 sixteen men at the signalbox at Warrington in the North-West on the main line to Scotland defied our instructions to work normally in a dispute over the classification of the new box. They would not stand in for colleagues who were off sick or on annual leave, and as a result there were widespread delays and disruption on the network. The men thought they were being underpaid for the work they were doing and they became impatient with the slowness with which their case was being examined in the industry's negotiating machinery.

We could not make special arrangements to improve the position of the Warrington signalmen. At the time we were reviewing the national deal that covered classification of all the big signalboxes and hoped to produce a better deal that would satisfy Warrington and everyone else, as in fact we finally did.

However, through much of 1979 these signalmen refused to carry out the instructions of the Executive Committee and work normally while their case was being examined. I made personal appeals to the signalmen but they ignored me. Special visits to the box by the union's divisional officer on my behalf were brushed aside. Meanwhile the London Midland Region of British Rail was sending me a stream of letters asking when we were going to honour the national agreement and deal with the rebel signalmen at Warrington.

I finally persuaded my Executive Committee to send for each of the signalmen involved. The idea was to advise them of their obligations to the union under the rules and warn that if they still refused to work normally after a specific time, the union through the Executive Committee would have no alternative but to take away their membership cards.

But before I proposed that course of action I had put the issue firmly to the Board's industrial relations director Clifford Rose that I would do nothing at all unless the Board agreed to sack every signalman who failed to carry out the union's instruction. Three weeks after my meeting with Rose to explain what I intended to do, he told me that the Board had agreed that if the NUR withdrew the membership cards of the signalmen, they would be dismissed for not complying with the industry's closed shop agreement.

I sent for the men two at a time for interviews at Head Office with Assistant General Secretaries Charlie Turnock and Frank Cannon together with some Executive members. The union rules were explained to them and they were asked if they understood them fully, then they were told that they would be expected to reply satisfactorily within a fortnight. My two assistants told me that these were the most difficult interviews they had ever carried out on behalf of the union, because many of the signalmen were longstanding NUR members with a record of loyal service. But they were all in serious breach of the rules.

I thought they were going to go on defying the union. But finally, just inside the fortnight deadline, a telegram arrived from Warrington on behalf of all the signalmen: 'We will carry out union instructions.' Not long afterwards their signalbox was reclassified in the way they had wanted in the first place, and I breathed a sigh of relief.

The Need for Trade Union Unity

The weakness of the TUC

I have always been a passionate believer in trade union unity. I know it is easy to say that and most union leaders only pay lip service to what it means, but throughout my life in the NUR I have seen at first hand the stupidity of trade unions competing inside the same industry. It hinders progress on every front. It prevents co-operation and understanding between management and workers. It stops the steady improvements in pay and working conditions that flow from a successful undertaking. We could have made much greater progress towards participation in management if we had had a single, united union throughout the industry. I have always been a strong believer in this principle of industrial unionism.

However great the advances made in working life and social conditions as a result of the advocacy and actions of the trade union movement, I can say without a shred of doubt that they would have been substantially greater if the trade unions had been more effectively organized.

The trouble really starts with the Trades Union Congress. I served on the General Council for eight years and sat on most of the key committees, but it was always clear to me that we were falling far short of being a coherent and well-disciplined force which no elected Government – not even that of Margaret Thatcher – could afford to ignore.

Some of the more farsighted TUC General Secretaries over the years argued for greater authority to be given to the TUC as the

112

representative voice of all Britain's trade unionists. Walter Citrine, General Secretary from the 1926 General Strike until just after the end of the Second World War, always wanted to see the TUC General Council as the general staff of Labour, with a clear sense of direction, taking on greater responsibilities for the welfare of working people and the management of the economy. In the 1960s George Woodcock had a vision of taking the TUC out of Trafalgar Square and into the corridors of Whitehall, where union leaders would have the authority and the power to get things done.

If only the movement had been bold enough to follow their ideas – but we have never really measured up to the formidable challenge that they declared. Len Murray certainly put the problems posed by his predecessors before the unions, though like them he has never really received any satisfactory answers from the movement. Every TUC General Secretary has a difficult task, and in no way do I underestimate his problem. He is bound to fudge issues because that is how the movement works. Often it seems to be the only way it can operate. It rubs me up the wrong way that this is so because I like things to be clear-cut. But that is the world of the TUC that we and he alike have to live in.

I have thought from time to time Murray underplayed the authority of his office. The flexible rostering dispute in 1982 is one instance I have in mind, when ASLEF deceived him and, after the TUC had saved the union from disaster, bit the hand that fed them. I wouldn't have Len Murray's job for all the tea in China.

In all my years on the TUC General Council I always had immense regard for the hard work carried out by the full-time staff in Congress House. The civil service of the trade union movement gets few accolades, but in their patient, diplomatic way Len Murray and his colleagues prepare papers and policies without much appreciation being shown for their efforts.

It is inside the committees that the real work of the TUC is done. We are provided with detailed documents, full of closely argued reasoning and suggested courses of action. Coping with the volume of material flowing through Congress House presents busy top union officers with a heavy task of digesting and understanding all the problems. Not all the members of the General Council serving on the committees are well briefed on their agendas. Some have been known to read their papers in their cars on the way to the meetings, including myself. In recent years, the sheer weight of work has led some union General Secretaries to make the TUC

113

almost their full-time preoccupation, while others spend little time on TUC work because of their other commitments. Most decisions reached in the TUC committees are endorsed by the full General Council without much debate.

There is no doubt that Congress House staff can ensure a steady progress of decision-making through the committee system. The backroom boys have a particular skill with words in the search for compromises.

On the last Wednesday of every month the General Council meets from ten in the morning to half past twelve, and it gets through the whole of a crowded agenda in that time. There is much more professional efficiency about the General Council's way of doing its business than in the Labour Executive Committee, which in my day was often an utter shambles with much less disciplined debates. At the General Council, everybody has a seat allocated at the table. When you are first elected you sit opposite the Chairman for the year and gradually, as you gain seniority, you move around the table. This stops factional groups from ganging up in certain parts of the table. When I was on the Labour Executive Committee, such cabals were commonplace.

Reform of the TUC's structure is vital if the trade union movement is to become more effective in representing the view of all Britain's trade unionists. But crucial to that development is a much greater unity of purpose inside the TUC itself. In the autumn of 1979 I believed the time was ripe to make some progress on an issue that has preoccupied the TUC on and off for most of its history, so I moved a resolution calling for an inquiry into the TUC's own structure.

We were facing what I believed to be the most reactionary Conservative government since the 1930s, but there was one clear difference between now and then. As I said at the 1979 Congress, 'In the thirties this movement was barely off its knees and was forced as a consequence to bow to the economic policies of that time.... [Now] no Government can govern Britain without our co-operation and our understanding.' I believed that Mrs Thatcher's Government would have to come to terms with us if we could achieve a greater centralized direction of strategy inside the TUC.

Unions affiliated to the TUC have to be willing to concentrate much more authority and power in the hands of the General Council so that it can work out the necessary strategy of action to defend the movement from Government attacks. Such a development would also allow the working out of a new policy of economic co-operation between the political and industrial wings of the Labour Party.

'We have so to organize the TUC and its powers that we can carry out to the full the policies about which we are agreed. In other words, we must be able to deliver any policies to which we put our name,' I told Congress in 1979. Unless Congress grasped this crucial issue the Government could rest content that the trade unions were not ready to do anything more to oppose Government policies than carry banners on street demonstrations and pass resolutions at union conferences.

My argument for greater power for the TUC General Council was not to the liking of many major trade union leaders, but they were wrong to think that maintaining their own trade union's autonomy, to do what the hell they liked without any thought for any other unions, gave them any more real influence on the course of events. I pointed out that at the 1978 Congress we had passed a motion without any opposition to press for a 35-hour working week without loss of earnings for workers. A document, *Employment and Technology*, was produced which spelt out the need to work for shorter hours and longer holidays. But the General Council backed away from the suggestion that it must establish priorities which might restrict the freedom of individual trade union negotiators by asking them to press those demands.

Yet, if we were really serious as a trade union movement about economic strategy and planning the nation's resources, we had to lay down what the priorities were and see they were carried out. 'Otherwise what are we here for?' I asked, echoing the famous words of General Secretary George Woodcock in the sixties. I wanted to see the General Council given the power from its member unions to change society in the direction we wanted. If we were opposed to going down such a road, we should say so – though if we did, the people we represented would know we were not serious about achieving our objectives.

As a result of the NUR motion at the 1979 Congress, the TUC set up an extensive review of its organization, structure and services. Two special conferences were held at Congress House in December 1980 and in April 1981, but very little of importance emerged from our discussions. This was mainly because the bigger unions in the movement continue to believe that there is nothing wrong with the

TUC as it is, and that no further powers should be assumed by the General Council because this would threaten the freedom of individual unions to pursue their own objectives.

What many outsiders don't realize is that the TUC is not separate and apart from affiliated unions, but can only act and speak for them with their consent. Any authority exercised by the TUC depends essentially on its ability to win the approval of a majority of its members – and a sizeable majority at that – for a proposed course of action. Rules and sanctions do have their place inside the TUC, but in reality their use must be sparing and exceptional. The TUC moves by consent through patient argument, or not at all.

Of course such slow, plodding work in the TUC can be exasperating for those like myself who want to see radical reform. I expressed my impatience about the lack of progress towards structural change at the 1980 Congress, when I moved a motion from my union that called for a reduction in the number of competing unions inside the same industry. There are fewer unions now than there used to be, but the movement is no more rationally organized today than it was half a century ago. The competitive attitude of unions to one another in the everlasting search for more members has sapped our strength. 'One of the greatest obstacles to change and improvement in Britain is this movement,' I told the Congress. 'There is no doubt that the way in which we have organized ourselves has a deterrent effect.' Every year over 100 internal union disputes are referred to the TUC to be sorted out, a clear sign of the basic weakness of the movement.

There should really be no more than about twenty trade unions in Britain, and they should be organized inside the TUC. My vision is of 12 million organized workers speaking in unison. 'The power that that voice would give us would astound us all,' I argued at the 1980 Congress. 'It would give us the power to sit in front of Governments and to exert influence on economic, social and international issues. No Government would dare not to meet us. If we were organized on that basis, our people would determine pay and conditions industry by industry and we would have more influence in managing the undertakings. Instead of the TUC General Council writing to the Prime Minister to ask whether we could see her, she would be knocking at our door and asking to come in and see us.'

I wasn't asking for the earth at the 1980 Congress, but at least I thought we could make some modest reforms. We might, for example, get much more uniformity in the TUC industrial committees. The Transport Industries Committee that I chaired had nine unions on it, while there were eleven unions on the Construction Committee, fourteen on the Health Services Committee and fourteen on the Steel Committee.

I was off on a journey to West Germany the following week to examine their trade union system. Here, what could be the new structure of British trade unionism already exists, and it works. That is my ideal for what can be done with the necessary commitment to change. Ironically, it was the TUC itself that played the main role in the creation of the West German trade union movement just after the Second World War.

Another major cause of weakness in the TUC stems from the lack of financial resources enjoyed by Congress House. We still have trade unionism on a shoestring in this country. Indeed, the TUC staggers from one financial problem to another. It was decided not to raise affiliation fees to the TUC in 1983, so that with declining memberships, rising expenditure and static income, the TUC faces a serious deficit over the next few years unless affiliate unions agree to cough up more money from their own stretched resources to meet the TUC's needs

The trouble, as always, is that unions like to keep their subscription rates low to make themselves more attractive to workers they want to recruit. The 'supermarket' mentality of many unions in constant competition with each other for membership ensures that the TUC cannot enjoy the realistic levels of income it must have if it hopes to become a much more effective national trade union centre like the West German or Swedish trade union movements.

Reforming the General Council

I have also been a strong supporter of the movement which took shape inside the TUC in the early 1980s to change the way in which the General Council was elected. The problem was that the big unions were able to use their powers of patronage to elect smaller unions, who were then virtually satellites ready to do as they were told. The train drivers' union ASLEF, for example, won a seat on the General Council on the Left-wing ticket in 1973 under the good offices of the TGWU, so whichever way the Transport Workers voted on crucial issues ASLEF was sure to follow. Buckton even supported the TGWU in voting against the idea of a Channel rail

Tunnel, although I would have thought it was plainly in the interest of all railwaymen that we should go ahead with the project.

The fiction of accountability of the General Council to the Congress has allowed the unseemly fixing of seats by the big unions to be clothed in a wholly misleading air of respectability. Important union leaders have been kept off the General Council because their faces or their politics failed to please the big union bosses. Communists such as the NUM leaders Will Paynter and Arthur Horner never won seats on the General Council, nor did Bryn Roberts of the National Union of Public Employees (NUPE), though he tried to get on for years. On the other hand, more moderate men such as Roy Grantham of the white-collar Association of Professional, Executive, and Clerical and Computer Staff (APEX) and Jack Peel of the Dyers and Bleachers were thrown off the General Council because they offended the big union bosses by opposing the ruling orthodoxies of the time.

Ganging up against certain individuals was a highly unpleasant feature of the old system. But there is an even deeper reason why the trade group-block vote approach met with my disapproval. It did not concentrate power at the centre of the TUC but gave it to a handful of trade union bosses with large block votes, and they were far keener on enjoying their own freedom of action than on agreeing to suggestions that a reformed General Council should be given greater power and responsibility.

Like mediaeval barons, they wanted to ensure that they held on to their privileges. It was only when first the General and Municipal Workers' Union (GMWU) and later the AUEW decided that the old system was indefensible that it became possible to get a majority in Congress to change it drastically, and even then we had to fight a long, uphill battle against delays and foot-dragging which may not yet be over. All trade unions in Britain with more than 100,000 members are now entitled to automatic representation on the General Council. There are to be 11 seats for the smaller unions in the TUC who will elect their representatives from among themselves, with the five women members left unchanged.

Automatic representation ends once and for all the myth of accountability, brings the selection procedure completely out into the open, and puts a stop to the wheeler-dealing of the Right and the Left which so disfigured the TUC in the past. I believe that in future the TUC General Council will be a much more representative body as a result of these long-overdue reforms. Unions with large and medium-sized memberships will not be excluded from the General Council by the arbitrary manipulation of block votes for the benefit of the few. The composition of the Council will give a more accurate reflection of the actual membership. For the first time the small unions will be sitting on the Council as of right and not because they are the vassals of a bigger union.

There was strong opposition to the changes, notably from the TGWU, revealing an unsavoury picture of indefensible vested interests fighting for their own survival. I was also convinced that there was a political motive behind the opposition to automatic representation. Under the trade group system, because some of the large unions were left-wing, the hard Left was able to enjoy a much greater presence on the General Council than its overall strength in the trade union movement could justify.

The new 53-strong Council is likely to prove a much more balanced and sensible body, less swayed by extreme Left-wing policies which could damage the trade union movement. The hatred of the Communist Party for what has been happening suggests that the Left is well aware of the longer-term political consequences of a more representative General Council, and this is why they are still fighting against the change.

Unfortunately many union leaders sometimes cannot rise above petty spite and their own ambitions when they work inside the TUC. I was made chairman of the transport industry committee when Jack Jones retired as General Secretary of the TGWU. For some time I had no reason to believe that my work did not meet with the approval of my colleagues, but I was to learn differently in September 1980.

There was a good deal of bitterness on the General Council that year over the behaviour of Frank Chapple, the tough General Secretary of the Electrical Electronic Telecommunication and Plumbing Union (EETPU). He had annoyed some union leaders including Moss Evans and especially David Basnett of the GMWU because of his outspoken criticisms of various decisions reached by the TUC. At one stage, Chapple – among others – almost found his union being expelled from the TUC for refusing to swallow a disputes committee award in a tricky inter-union wrangle at the Isle of Grain power station.

I don't agree with all that Frank Chapple says, but you know where he stands. He has seen at first hand from his days in the

Communist Party those elements in our society which are seeking to destroy democratic institutions, and how they operate. And because he exposes them for what they are they attack him constantly. He operates from a sound power base in his union, and consequently he treats his opponents with contempt.

By 1980 he was a senior figure on the TUC General Council, where he had sat for ten years. He had reached the inner ruling group, but the big union leaders suddenly ganged up against him and threw him off the TUC's Finance and General Purposes Committee, the Cabinet of the organization. This happened on the TUC Committee which meets once a year immediately after each Congress to make all the appointments to the Committees.

I thought this was a serious mistake and I said so publicly. The trade union movement should exercise tolerance, good manners and mutual respect. If we started to penalize people on the General Council because we disagreed with their opinions or attitudes, then we might as well be cardboard cut-out figures, devoid of thought or feelings and with no room for prejudices or occasional stupidity. If power in the TUC was going to be used to try to force everybody to conform to the majority opinion whatever that might be, we ought to resist it.

Little did I know but I was going to be the next to suffer. Committee chairmen usually keep their position, but at the first meeting of the transport committee after Congress I was not only voted out of the chair by a majority there but was replaced by a man – Larry Smith of the TGWU – who had only recently been elected to the General Council. The vote was 12 to 7 against me, with Buckton of ASLEF amongst the twelve. There was much talk in the press at that time of a purge of the TUC by the hard Left and a 'night of the long knives'. Moss Evans rang me up to say there had been some terrible mistake and if only he had been at the meeting he would have proposed I should stay on as chairman, but I also heard that Evan's deputy, the Left-wing Alex Kitson, was behind the move to restore the TGWU to a position the union thought it ought to have, almost as of right.

I did not know whom to believe, but all I know is that I did not get my job back as chairman of the transport committee. I raised the issue on the General Council at its next meeting but Alan Fisher of NUPE ruled me out of order, saying it was up to each committee of the TUC alone to decide who should be its chairman. The whole business left a nasty taste in my mouth and wrecked the efforts I had been making to establish much closer and friendlier relations with the TGWU. We had been working together through the International Transport Workers' Federation on transport problems in Europe, but now relations between us remained sour for some time as a result of their stab in the back.

I thought the dropping of Chapple and then my downfall was part of a plot to purge moderate voices from key positions in the TUC. There were fears that Tom Jackson of the Post Office Workers would be the next to lose his post as chairman of the international committee, and Bill Sirs of the Iron and Steel Trades Confederation (ISTC) was believed to be vulnerable as well. In the event, neither of these things happened. A year later Chapple got his seat back on the Finance and General Purposes Committee and he became president of the TUC for September 1982-September 1983. But the whole episode did not do the reputation of the TUC any good.

The Triple Alliance and Scargill

By 1980 the TUC was clearly fighting a losing battle in its efforts to persuade Mrs Thatcher's Government to change course. Meetings between leaders of the TUC and the Prime Minister proved to be totally futile. She lectured us on her simple-minded economic ideas and hardly concealed her contempt for what we had to say. We were not on the same wavelength. But while the TUC was unable to make the Government see sense in its economic policies, these were having a devastating effect on the country's basic industries, particularly those that were nationalized. Sitting together on the TUC nationalized industries committee with thirty-six other unions, I began to realize that the fortunes of the railways were closely linked to those of the steel and coal industries.

Joe Gormley, the NUM President, and Bill Sirs of the ISTC recognized this as well, so we decided to come together and try to hammer out a common policy and programme of action. We were all suffering from the financial restrictions imposed by the Government and if one of our industries went to the wall, the other two would surely follow. In fact, we were interdependent. Railways were moving 70 per cent of the coal produced by the Coal Board, and had substantial business with the steel industry.

I had a good relationship with both Gormley and Sirs. They always delivered what they said they would. Their word was good enough for me. Both were political animals in the sense that they

121

were long standing Labour Party members and they were totally loyal to the movement, but they were never prepared to use their members as political cannon fodder. I found a common bond with them because we shared the same outlook on politics and trade unionism.

The thirteen-week national steel strike in 1980 had helped to stimulate a greater need for us to work together in the common cause. I suggested to Gormley and Sirs that without wishing to cut out the TUC's involvement it might be to our advantage if we could formulate a joint policy and not only pursue this within Britain but also advocate it in the European Economic Community. I saw that coal, steel and rail worked together harmoniously on the Continent, and it seemed to me we could achieve the same benefits of partnership here. The three of us decided to establish a properly-based trade union alliance with clear-cut objectives.

We agreed that this 'Triple Alliance' should be confined to the three main unions in the industry, for if we let a larger number of unions become involved this would have made it harder to reach decisions. The troubles that existed between unions in the steel industry and on the railways were much in our minds.

It was also made very clear that we would be calling on assistance for each other only on major issues. The shutdown of one pit or the closure of one depot would not be the sort of problems that would be considered of sufficient magnitude. We met together for the first time for a joint conference on 23 January 1981 at the Great Western Hotel at Paddington station with Joe Gormley in the chair. Representatives from other unions in the mining, steel and railway industries were invited along as observers. The idea was not to seek any political confrontation, but reasoned argument based upon cold economic analysis of the problems facing the three industries.

We produced a joint policy statement, *What is the Future?*, which set out our common strategy. There were to be no further closures of steel capacity, particularly of the big five steelmaking plants, and we promised to take whatever action was necessary to defend jobs in those plants. We also said there must be no closure of pits on purely economic grounds, and we called for Government protection against coal and steel imports as well as State subsidies to preserve existing production levels.

As for the railways, all three unions pledged themselves to fight for 'increased support for passenger services, a firm commitment to

122

large-scale electrification to improve the quality of service and a steady increase in the amount of investment funds available to modernize and re-equip the railway system'. We called for Government approval of the plan for a single rail tunnel under the Channel.

Shortly afterwards we arranged a meeting between the Alliance and the senior Ministers for the three industries, with Jim Prior, then Employment Secretary, taking the chair. We presented our policy and had a frank exchange of views. Prior indicated we should meet again if it was found necessary. We now set about creating joint working arrangements in local areas. The Alliance seemed to be making progress.

Then Joe Gormley announced that he would retire early in 1982 and there was a heavy blow to the future of the Alliance: the election of Arthur Scargill as President of the NUM in November 1981. I found it impossible to work with him.

I had met Scargill only once before he arrived in London as the Mineworkers' President. This was in Yorkshire in December 1980 when we went down Kellingley pit together. I found him a strange man and difficult to understand. He spent much of the time talking to men at the coalface, running down the way Joe Gormley had conducted the recent pay negotiations for the miners. When I questioned him about this and his loyalty towards the miners' Executive decisions he brushed my queries aside, saying he was President of the Yorkshire Miners and was free to disagree with his union's policies. I soon realized I was dealing with somebody I felt was much less reliable than Joe Gormley.

Scargill soon wrecked the Triple Alliance. On 24 May 1982 he wrote to me suggesting that there should be a reconvened conference to discuss the Tory threat to our industries and the advent of new technology, and he said that he had written to Buckton, Arthur Simpson of the miners' supervisory union, NACODS, and Hector Smith of the Blastfurnacemen (NUB) inviting them along not as observers, but as full-scale representatives.

I replied at once, expressing my surprise at his behaviour in contacting unions which were not part of the Triple Alliance to propose another conference without consulting us. I suggested that he should meet Bill Sirs and myself before any further steps were to taken to reconvene the conference as he planned. Bill Sirs wrote to him on similar lines.

Then Scargill again acted contrary to what I saw as the spirit

123

and intention of the Triple Alliance when his union decided to give financial support to ASLEF in its idiotic strike over flexible rostering. But when I tried to contact him to get the NUM to support our strike in July 1982 I couldn't even find him or get him to return my call, so I sent out circulars to the area offices of his union to inform them of our industrial action and ask for their backing. By the end of August relations between Scargill and myself, were, to say the least, strained.

On 1 September he sent me an extraordinary letter in which he complained that I had flagrantly disregarded his union's constitution by contacting the area offices of the Mineworkers. Apparently he did not like my suggestion that he had been a 'reluctant militant' in our dispute. He further claimed that the TUC had been guilty of a 'betrayal' of ASLEF during the flexible rostering dispute. 'All those who contributed to undermining the ASLEF dispute will have to answer both to their memberships and to their consciences for failing to support a trade union in their fight against both an employer and a Tory government,' he wrote to me, and added that he was sending a copy of his letter to every member of my Executive Committee.

I wrote back to put the record straight: 'I must state my strong resentment at the steps you took to assist ASLEF without first ascertaining the views of the NUR, serving the preponderance of employees in the railway industry. True, ASLEF were in dispute with an employer, but that was no reason why you should not consider the NUR and the effect the dispute was having on its members. How would you feel if I supported NACODS [the mining overseers' union] in a mining dispute without first consulting you?'

I then explained to Scargill in plain language what the flexible rostering strike had been about: 'The facts of the recent rail dispute were that it never was an issue of trying to destroy a union. It was from start to finish the narrow issue of flexible rostering together with the repeated failure by a trade union to honour agreement after agreement, commitment after commitment, not simply with the Railways Boards but with ACAS and also with the TUC General Secretary and fellow unionists in the railway industry. The TUC's inner cabinet were quite right to denounce the anti-trade-union attitude of ASLEF. Trade-union and working-class loyalty does not mean that the movement gives support to selfish, stupid strikes staged by small unrepresentative groups in a particular industry. It is an insult to the movement to ask for support and an even greater insult to condemn fellow trade unionists if they failed to respond. It is a sad day for the labour and trade union movement when the train drivers' leadership pour out their venom in this way, thus debasing the status of the whole trade union movement.'

That was the last I heard from him. With Scargill in charge of the Mineworkers, the hopes of the Triple Alliance faded. Since my resignation efforts have been made to revive the Alliance and it has been extended to cover more unions, including ASLEF, but the bigger it is the less effective it will be, and if it is turned into a hard-Left organization, which is Scargill's objective, the members will not take any notice of what it says.

The Rail Federation

My union is dedicated to the principles of industrial unionism. It says on the front cover of the rulebook issued to every member that the NUR is 'a union of railway and ancillary workers of all grades united to advance their social conditions. United also for mutual aid and protection.'

That simple message is as clear and apt today as it was when the union was founded in 1913. But the railway industry has long been plagued with inter-union rivalry.

In my younger days the strength of the NUR lay in the solidarity of all grades of railwaymen in the depressed areas of south Wales, Scotland and the North-East of England, where they knew that if you were not standing together shoulder to shoulder in one union you were cut to ribbons. It was in the more prosperous Southern and Western regions where ASLEF made the most progress. The train-drivers' union has always had a majority in those areas because the mentality was different and the 'I'm all right Jack' philosophy prevailed. But since the war affluence has created a different approach in all parts of the country. There came to be more Labour voters but fewer Socialists, and when there were fewer Socialists there were fewer trade unionists who believed in industrial unionism.

Long before I was elected General Secretary I realized that the aim of one union for the railways was in danger of remaining an impossible dream, because the smaller unions, ASLEF and TSSA, were frightened of being swallowed up inside my union. So I accepted that initially the best we could hope for was the creation of a loose federation between the three of us with joint national executives and a joint annual conference, but also an agreed autonomy for each affiliate in a broad structure. Each union would enjoy a veto power in the federation so that no controversial decisions could be steam-rollered through against the opposition of one of the partners.

Over the years I had many battles with ASLEF, but personally I had nothing against Ray Buckton. I have always had the impression that he was very much controlled by his Executive. He never came to meetings without the ASLEF President at his shoulder, seemingly acting as a minder. We had no personal contact and during all my eight years as NUR General Secretary I only once went to ASLEF's headquarters in Hampstead. Our relations tended to be stiff and formal, punctuated by mutual acrimony, although this was not a personal quarrel between two argumentative Yorkshiremen as portrayed in the media. Rivalries and tensions between the NUR and ASLEF run deep in the railway industry, and they will not be easily overcome.

Nevertheless I was keen – especially after the pay train guard farce I have already discussed – to make a move towards unity with the rail unions. The catalyst for this was a bitter row we had with ASLEF over its poaching some of our members on London Transport. I reported this to the TUC, but subsequent talks made no progress at all. Then I took the initiative to break the deadlock. I asked Buckton and his President to a meeting at Unity House on 12 June 1979. I proposed that his union should come to an agreement with us, whereby ASLEF stopped recruitment in London Transport and we in return would cease recruiting footplatemen employed by British Rail. They both showed interest, but subsequently their Executive would have none of this. Instead it suggested that ASLEF would limit its recruitment at London Transport to guards and motormen only. I did not think that that was any kind of compromise or give-or-take. However, I did not give up my efforts. I brought in Len Murray to try to help us achieve the Federation.

Progress was painfully slow but we drafted a new constitution for the proposed body. Unfortunately our union conference in Jersey in 1980 would have none of it.

Between 1919 and our 1980 annual conference debate we had had eighteen debates on the need for one big rail union, but the argument for that had never been won. However, we had not discussed a Federation before and I thought the delegates would

126

back this as the important first step to the unity we all wanted. Since my election in 1975 it had been a rough five years, I told the 1980 conference. 'Not between Buckton and me, but between the basic principles on which this union stands against sectionalism which says preferential treatment for certain grades. This is the battle which I waged on your behalf to say that no grade in this industry is going to get preferential treatment as long as I am General Secretary, because they are in a separate union.' The prize I was after was the formation of a Railway Trade Union Federation with a constitution drawn up by the TUC, tight and tough, which nobody could renege on. It would be a federal arrangement, where each union would be committed to see that it worked. If it got started, I thought we might move within five years to one union for all railway workers, although that was not explicit in the proposals. However, many of my activist members did not like the idea of a federalist approach. They believed that ASLEF could not survive on its own for much longer. But even if they were right, there was no guarantee that the train drivers would come and join us.

In any case my arguments failed to carry the day and delegates voted by a massive 61 votes to 12 to reject my approach. Len Murray was, however, in no mood to give up his efforts by that stage. 'You may have finished with it as an Executive Committee but I have not finished with it as General Secretary of the TUC,' he told me. 'I am going to try and find a solution.'

Eventually, after many months of discussion, in 1981 we reached an agreement, which looked at the time like a breakthrough and contained a commitment to the eventual emergence of one union for the industry. My conference then backed it and we signed the deal in September. Both sides, together with Len Murray, also signed an agreement on trade union membership and representation to overcome the difficulties at London Transport. We agreed to stop staff recruitment among workers in line for promotion to train driver on British Rail, and we were to encourage transfer to ASLEF of our members in those grades on British Rail. In return ASLEF agreed to transfer certain categories of London Transport staff to our membership.

The way was now open for growing co-operation between our two unions at every level. The new agreement put a stop to the bitter contests that had been fought between NUR and ASLEF nominees down at the depots in the sectional council elections. I hoped that we could now put behind us the fears and mistrust which had prevented the first constructive move towards one union.

But lamentably, troubles continued. ASLEF began to jump the gun by taking in many of our members without even telling us. The drivers' union was misusing the agreement which had just been signed to poach for our members on London Transport. About fifty of our members moved to ASLEF as a result.

I quickly realized that the ASLEF leaders were not taking the Rail Federation idea at all seriously. In a speech in Manchester Buckton suggested there 'could never be one union for all railway workers' and he argued that the Federation guaranteed ASLEF's sole future negotiating rights with British Rail, something he had been fighting to achieve for years.

I was not proposing that the new Federation was to be just a talking shop. I saw us going together as one body to the negotiating table to meet management as a united team in 1982. We had agreed on a joint Executive Committee for the new organization, and on its size and its composition. We had agreed the dates in 1982 on which that joint Executive Committee should meet, and worked out the size and powers of a joint annual conference. We even went as far as accepting that the first annual conference should meet in ASLEF headquarters in Arkwright Road as a gesture of solidarity.

Now Buckton and his Executive were simply exploiting our goodwill to further the narrow interests of their own union. A month later in October 1982 – despite signing an agreement that said we would co-ordinate and unify our policies – ASLEF decided to call a strike over cuts in passenger services, without even bothering to tell us. Two months later they decided to strike over flexible rostering without breathing a word to the NUR beforehand.

On issue after issue we bent over backwards to please ASLEF, and we received nothing but insults in return. I was so exasperated about what was going on that finally I wrote to Len Murray early in January 1982, asking him to convene a meeting at Congress House between the two rail unions to discuss the lack of progress on the Federation. Buckton and his new President, Derek Fullick, turned up with accusations against me for allegedly breaking the spirit and letter of the Federation. They laid out their charges in front of Murray, who then asked me what I thought about what they were saying.

I told him: 'I have never heard so many lies in my life.' At that point Fullick leaned across the table and said he would 'put one' on me for those remarks. (Later it was wrongly reported that he had threatened to throw me down the lift shaft at Congress House.) Murray managed to calm everyone down, but I was very angry at ASLEF's militant antics, which showed no regard at all for the painstaking negotiations we had held over at least two years to establish a federal understanding between the two rail unions.

In fact, the disputes of 1982 suggested that the Federation agreement we signed had not been worth the paper it was printed on. ASLEF had not changed its old ways at all and I felt I had been taken for a ride. Every clause in the agreement was tossed out of the window.

At the 1982 annual conference in Plymouth I said of Buckton that he spewed out what he was told to say by the ASLEF Executive Committee: 'Our problem is to find within this society, not only in railways, in management and in politics, how people can sit down and talk and reach agreement and work and live together.'

It will be interesting to see how the Rail Federation develops, if at all, over the next few years. But I know that my departure has made no fundamental difference to a genuine problem. 'Even if Mr Buckton disappears and Mr Weighell disappears, the world will not change dramatically,' I told my union's delegates. 'You will get rid of two Yorkshiremen, I agree, but whether you will get better in their places I do not know.'

Fighting to Save the Labour Party

No trade union played a greater part in the creation of the Labour Party than the NUR. The parent body of the union – the old Amalgamated Society of Railway Servants – sponsored the original TUC resolution in 1899 at the Plymouth Congress which led to the creation of the Labour Representation Committee the following year. The union was one of the first two to affiliate to the Committee, which in 1906 was converted into the Labour Party.

Events concerning the union also provided the stimulus for a widespread move among the rest of the trade union movement to affiliate to the new organization. In 1901 the Taff Vale railway company attacked the union and gained verdicts in the courts against the ASRS which appeared to threaten the legal security of the whole trade union movement.

The NUR has remained an integral part of the Labour movement, and is dedicated to democratic Socialism. In the words of our constitution, we are working for 'the supersession of the capitalist system by a Socialistic order of society'. The principles of democracy and Socialism have been linked inextricably together and I have always seen the Labour Party as their practical expression.

The years I had spent on Labour's National Executive Committee had given me an insight into the party, and when I became General Secretary I was determined to strengthen the political profile of the NUR both inside the Labour movement and in Parliament itself. For many years we had not made our presence as a union felt where it mattered. I planned to change that.

Before Crosland's controversial paper on transport in 1976 our union-sponsored MPs were not well organized and we hardly ever saw them. They used to amble along to meet our political sub-committee every six months for lunch and an informal chat. But Crosland inadvertently provided a great stimulus to revive the group, and the NUR parliamentary group of Labour MPs subsequently became one of the most active of such bodies at Westminster.

The first innovation I made was to appoint a political liaison officer in June 1976. Keith Hill, a researcher from the Labour Party international department, and who had for three years been a lecturer in politics at Strathclyde University, took the job. He kept the closest contact between the union and our sponsored MPs in a post that was at first unique in the trade union world. The new links proved very successful in our campaign against the Crosland Consultation Document. We began to organize the NUR MPs in raising questions in the House of Commons on railway topics, arguing the case for expansion and new investment. They lobbied against the threat of cuts to the network and the suggestion that buses could replace trains on rural services. They played an important part in pressing the Government for railway electrification, the building of a Channel tunnel and the introduction of new rolling stock. Transport Secretary Bill Rodgers owned that the NUR had the most effective trade union group in the House of Commons.

At my first annual conference as General Secretary I got delegates to agree to an expansion in the size of the NUR parliamentary group so we could use the expertise of Labour MPs who were not members of the NUR but had a knowledge of industry and transport that would assist our cause. As a result we recruited four unsponsored MPs into the group – Tam Dalyell (West Lothian); Robin Cook (Edinburgh Central); Philip Whitehead (Derby North) and Donald Anderson (Swansea East). Later on the able Scottish MP Donald Dewar (South Aberdeen) joined the group as well. I was able to say in my first political report to the annual conference in 1978: 'Thanks largely to the concerted campaign by the union and our MPs there has been a transformation in the outlook for railways in the past two years.'

At the 1975 annual conference we had also agreed to try to increase the political awareness of our members by making NUR affiliation to constituency Labour Parties compulsory. The mere change of rule did not mean, of course, that the union branch automatically sent delegates along to the general management committee of their local Labour party, but our more active involvement in political affairs helped to give the NUR a louder voice, where it mattered.

The union took a prominent part in the May 1979 general election campaign. As soon as the date of the election was announced the NUR Executive Committee donated some £45,000 to the Labour Party's general election fund. On top of that, we provided £20,000 to meet the election expenses of our NUR-sponsored parliamentary candidates. Only one of the twelve failed to win a parliamentary seat in the general election.

Mrs Thatcher's victory was a disaster for the Labour movement, and not just because of the loss of the election. Afterwards I hoped that the party and the unions would quickly work out new and sensible policies to combat the Tories, building on the Social Contract to establish a closer working partnership between the two wings of the Labour movement. But instead we lurched into some of the most bitter internal conflicts in the party's history, which threatened to destroy Labour's credibility as a party able to govern the country.

By the spring of 1980 I was becoming increasingly concerned at the infiltration of the party by hard-Left organizations, most notably the Militant Tendency. These zealots have a contempt for parliamentary democracy and they form a cancerous growth inside the Labour movement. If it is not cut out, the party will gradually die. I decided that we must call for drastic action to purge the party of those elements as quickly as possible. Otherwise there was little hope that Labour could remain a credible political party and win back power.

To combat the threat, our 1980 annual conference decided to demand the return of the proscribed list of organizations banning members of any of these dangerous bodies from membership of the party. The idea of the proscribed list went back to the early 1930s when the Communist Party was trying to infiltrate Labour's ranks. The National Executive Committee was given the power at that time to draw up a list of organizations which were considered to be incompatible with party membership. Proper procedures were established so that the accused had the right of appeal to the party conference before any expulsion was carried out.

The basis of this effort to sever the links between the Labour Party and other Leftist political bodies was entirely above-board and legitimate. The party constitution, drawn up in 1918, states that organizations with 'their own programme, principles and policy for distinctive and separate propaganda' or 'possessing branches in the constituencies or engaged in the promotion of parliamentary or local government candidatures or owing allegiance to any political organization situated abroad' are not eligible to be affiliated to Labour. It would be a strange political party that was not prepared to protect itself from infiltration by outside bodies opposed to its basic aims and objectives.

But in 1973, when I was a member of the National Executive Committee, we decided to end the list of proscribed organizations. The main reason for this was that the list was completely out of date, consisting mainly of Communist-front bodies that no longer existed or existed in name only. However, we did not take the view that the existence of a proscribed list itself was mistaken. Rather, our report stated that the list had given rise to confusion: 'The existence of a list had created an impression that if an organization was not listed it was in order for affiliated and party associations to associate with it.' At the same time we drew attention to Clause Two of the party constitution which said that it was the duty of every general management committee of local constituency parties 'to take all necessary steps to safeguard the constitution, programme, principles and policy of the Labour Party within the constituency'.

The ending of the proscribed list, in other words, did not represent a sudden change of policy towards tolerating extremist or subversive organizations inside the party, but acknowledged that safeguards already existed in Labour's constitution to keep out the lunatic fringe. Our statement actually urged all affiliated and party bodies to 'continue to refrain from associating with other political organizations whose aims and objects [were] not consistent with those of the Labour Party'.

But although the principle was clear, in practice the change led to a great deal of confusion. In the absence of any clear guidelines from the National Executive Committee, constituency parties and their officers were simply at a loss to know what was or was not an organization compatible with party membership.

By the mid-1970s influential elements began to congregate around Tony Benn, airing the ridiculous opinion that anybody could join the party, no matter what kind of Left-wing political views they had. The hard-Left majority on the National Executive simply refused to back requests made by local constituency parties that certain individuals should be expelled because they acted contrary to the conditions of Labour membership.

In the summer of 1980 we had reached the crazy situation where people in the party were making clear their root and branch opposition to everything Labour stood for and nobody was doing anything about it. The antics of the National Executive Committee amounted to putting out the 'welcome' mat to all sorts of elements hostile to democratic Socialism.

I had the Militant Tendency chiefly in mind. It was clear to me, and anybody else who cared to look for themselves, that the extremist group was a party inside the party, complete with its own newspaper, full-time organizers, cells, training schools and ample funds. The National Executive Committee refused to do anything about the evidence of extremist infiltration compiled by Labour's former national agent Reg Underhill, and indeed they suppressed any publication of what the inquiry had found out.

We had to draw the line somewhere if the party was to be saved from extremism. I have been smeared with accusations of McCarthyism, but I am not in favour of witch-hunts. I simply believe that any democratic party has a right to protect itself from those who want to use it for other purposes. There have always been more or less formal groupings inside the Labour Party, whether of the Left, Right or Centre, and there is nothing wrong with that as long as they are committed to the parliamentary road to Socialism and they operate quite openly and democratically within the party without any secret cells and funds.

However, in 1980 the proscribed list approach was an emotive issue inside the party and I reckoned there was little chance of achieving its immediate reintroduction. I thought it better at that stage to broaden the awareness among the party members about the threat we all faced. In my view, the best strategy was to give such organizations as the Militant Tendency enough rope to hang themselves.

I wanted to see the National Executive Committee furnished with full details of all groups that wanted to organize inside the party. They would be expected to give information on their activities, their membership, their finances and their publications. It would then be up to the National Executive Committee to decide which of the organizations were compatible with party membership and which were not. If any organization refused to provide the information, its members were to be expelled from the party. Two years later I am glad to say that Labour came round to my way of thinking, but it was terribly late in the day.

The NUR's efforts to raise the issue of the proscribed list at the 1981 party conference failed to gain much support. Only the ISTC was ready at that time to back our demands. The conference arrangements committee ruled that the issue should not be debated but instead remitted to the party Executive. I challenged the decision at the start of the conference, pointing out that the combined vote of the NUR and the Steelmen totalled over 300,000, which was almost equal to the total membership of the constituency Labour parties, but the platform would have none of it. Nevertheless, the party Executive of 1981 did decide to look at the Militant issue.

My union was not content just to take the offensive against the termites inside the party. We were also determined to make Labour a much broader-based party whose Executive Committee and annual conference would more accurately reflect the views of ordinary rank-and-file and Labour voters, and not be so prone to the machinations of extremists.

The commission of inquiry which had been set up in 1979 to look at Labour's structure was something that I took seriously. I insisted that the union carried out its own thorough investigation of Labour's organization and made proposals as to how it might be reformed. We published our report in April 1980 under the title *Towards a New Compact for Labour*, and it was presented to the party's commission of inquiry for their study.

We proposed the creation of a new full-time financial officer for the party who was to be professionally qualified, enjoying a status similar to that of National Agent. We also backed the idea of State funding of political parties. (Later, in 1980-81, I sat on a commission which was set up by the Hansard Society and chaired by Edmund Dell which also came down in favour of State aid to the parties.) My union – unlike most others – made the maximum contribution possible to the constituency parties, and we suggested that all organizations should be obliged to pay out the maximum amount for sponsored candidates and MPs.

But our main proposals concerned changes in the structure of the party. The Labour Party conference has become a parody of policy-making, often passing mutually contradictory motions, but nevertheless the party's MP's are required to carry out its decisions in Parliament, and it is they themselves who are roundly condemned if those policies prove to be unworkable.

A credible Labour Party programme can only be assembled on the basis of a genuine, thoroughgoing debate and democratic consensus within the party, and that is not possible under the present system. We proposed that one day of the party conference each year should be devoted to two major policy areas for serious discussion in depth, which would get us away from the sloganizing and superficiality that passes for debate at present.

Detailed documents on the areas chosen by the National Executive Committee should be drawn up and go through widespread discussion at constituency and regional party level before coming to the annual conference. The more people are involved in drawing up the policy, the better chance there is that it will be practicable, and it will enjoy much greater credibility among Labour supporters than at present.

We also wanted to see a drastic reform of the National Executive Committee. It ought to contain a powerful and sensibly balanced representation of the trade unions, the constituency parties and MPs. In fact it is notable for the absence of genuine grassroots representatives and the virtual absence of elected representatives of the MPs. In 1981 as many as 19 of the NEC's 28 members were MPs, but only two of them were in any sense elected as their representatives by Labour MPs. These were Michael Foot, the leader, and his deputy Denis Healey. The rest were seats allocated to constituencies, the unions or women. As a result the NEC is at one and the same time top-heavy with Members of Parliament and yet unrepresentative of the parliamentary party as such.

The urgent need is to restrict membership of the NEC's constituency party section to authentic grassroots representatives, who should not be either MPs or trade union officials. I argued that there should be one from each of the 11 regional groupings in the party, elected by delegates who go to the regional conferences.

At the same time we thought that MPs themselves should have their own direct representation on the NEC. There would be seven of them elected by the parliamentary party including the leader and deputy leader. My union also favoured a seat each for the Young Socialists, the Socialist societies, local councillors and women. This would entail cutting the women's section down from its present five. The twelve trade union seats would stay as they were. I submitted a resolution on these lines to the 1982 party conference, and the Executive gave it their favourable consideration.

Adoption of these proposals would make Labour a much more democratic party, with an effective voice for all sections in policy-making. Unfortunately the Bennite Left at that time had their own limited ideas of how the party should be reformed from within. They wanted to make only modest changes, and those with the effect of giving them a better chance to dominate the party.

At the Bishop's Stortford summit conference of the party in August 1980 Jim Callaghan made an error fatal to the cause of party unity when he agreed to a change in the method of electing the party leader. Up to that time the decision had always been left to the Labour MPs, but now the Left majority on the party Executive wanted to 'extend the franchise' so that the constituency parties and the trade unions should also have a direct say in who should lead the party.

The 1980 Labour Party conference in Blackpool proved to be an almost complete triumph for the hard Left. A final attempt to oppose the compulsory reselection of Labour MPs failed. More significantly, the delegates also voted by a narrow margin of 98,000 votes to support a change in the system of electing the party leader and deputy leader. The moderate unions were completely outmanoeuvred by the Bennite forces. It looked as though the party was undergoing a revolution.

The party conference had decided that a special conference should be held in January to decide on the exact composition of the new electoral college for choosing the leader and deputy leader. Three weeks after Blackpool Callaghan resigned as leader and, in the last contest to be fought by the old method of decision by Labour MPs alone, Michael Foot defeated Denis Healey.

We decided to call a special conference of our own to decide what the NUR should do at the special Labour conference, which was to be held at Wembley. The union met on the Monday before the Wembley conference and decided by a substantial majority to go for the formula that would provide Labour MPs with half the votes in a postal electoral college, while the rest were evenly divided between the constituency parties and the trade unions. Personally I should have preferred to keep the old system, as the suggested electoral college would create far greater room for division inside the party and prove a much more inflexible and time-consuming method of electing Labour's leader and deputy leader.

I spoke at that eventful conference in the Wembley conference centre on 24 January 1981 and left nobody in any doubt where my union stood on the issue. I criticized the party's National Executive Committee for the way in which it was manipulating the constitution for its own purposes. At both the 1978 and the 1979 party conferences, efforts to change the method of electing the leader and deputy leader by 'extending the franchise' had been defeated. Even in 1980 it had only, as I said, been 'scrambled...though by a wafer-thin majority'. I went on to say that the party Executive committee 'spewed out claptrap' about democracy in the unions and how the conference was the sole arbiter of Labour policy when they meant that they favoured this as long as conference decisions were ones they agreed with.

I reminded the delegates of the proposals on reform of the party constitution that the NUR had made to the commission of inquiry into making Labour's National Executive Committee more representative of the views of the parliamentary party and the ordinary rank and file. And I had some strong words to say about the way the party conference functioned. 'The way we conduct our business here is not democratic,' I argued. 'We come here, we have a gaggle of composites pointing in ten different directions on issues like world peace or economic policy. We dispose of them in thirty minutes. Then somebody says that is the decision and the governing policy to be followed out by Parliament. They do not know which decision to pick up first.'

I went on to criticize the use of the trade union block vote to decide the outcome of any leadership elections. In my view, the postal electoral college was a rational and sensible arrangement that you could check. In this way we could avoid any suggestions of electoral fiddling. But the Wembley conference was in no mood to listen to rational arguments. We went through a series of eliminating ballots to decide on the new electoral system. The party's National Executive's proposal to give a third of the votes each to Labour MPs, constituency parties and trade union block votes failed to carry the day, but so did the 50-25-25 formula that my union was backing.

Thanks to a good deal of manipulation and scheming behind the scenes by the hard Left in the Bennite Rank and File Mobilizing Committee, the conference opted for a plan put up by the Union of Shop, Distributive and Allied Workers (USDAW). This gave the trade union block votes 40 per cent of the votes in the new electoral

college, with 30 per cent each to the Labour MPs and the consti-
tuency parties. It was a disastrous Saturday's work, and on the
next day three prominent party members – Shirley Williams,
David Owen and Bill Rodgers – signed the so-called Limehouse
Declaration which led on to the formation of the Social Democratic
Party two months later.

I did not support those who broke away from the Labour Party. I
thought they should have stayed and fought inside Labour's ranks
for what they believed to be right. They were splitting the anti-
Tory forces and weakening the democratic Left in Britain.

The emergence of the new party also made it much harder for
more sensible people in the Labour movement to win the fight back
against the forces of extremism. Yet here the tide was already
beginning to turn in some of the key unions early in 1981, notably
in the AUEW whose President Terry Duffy had routed the Broad
Left. We had every hope of making substantial gains on the
National Executive Committee in the autumn elections.

I did not take the hard-Left view that those who joined the Social
Democrats from Labour's ranks were traitors to the working class.
Indeed, I was sad to see many of them go because I believe their
departure was a genuine loss to the credibility and effectiveness of
the Labour Party. But I remain convinced that the only real
alternative to the Conservatives lies in the Labour movement,
with unions and party working together in the common interest of
working people. In the midst of the worst slump since the 1930s
and faced with a reactionary Government the like of which had not
been seen for many generations, I believed that we should work
together for unity and not weaken ourselves by self-destructive
conflicts or adopting hard-Left policies that stood no chance of
gaining majority support through the ballot box.

By the time of our annual conference in 1981 at St Andrews I had
become the prime trade union target for the hard Left because of
my belligerent attacks on their activities. In my political report to
the delegates I wrote: 'After a period of covert activity [the infiltra-
tors] now feel themselves well enough entrenched to proclaim
quite openly their Trotskyist and revolutionary allegiances....
We should be in no doubt about their determination to convert the
Labour party into a Bolshevik-style organization paving the way
to physical confrontation on the streets. With such people there can
be no compromise, there can be no hope of genuine unity in the
party. That is why the NUR has proposed that the party should

139

now take the measures necessary to protect itself from those who would destroy it. Resolute action will be required.'

I am more than ever convinced that the voters of Britain will not tolerate Trotskyist fantasies, and that they will not elect the Labour Party to power where such views have the upper hand. It was a tragedy that at this time not enough people recognized the growing danger, and when eventually they did, took so long and did so little to counter it.

There followed months of self-destructive mayhem caused by Tony Benn in his raging campaign to become deputy leader of the party. I never had much time for him. I saw him as an aristocratic Socialist, born with a silver spoon in his mouth. He puts on a show of sweetness and light, like a country vicar, but he associates with political extremists. He drinks tea out of a pint pot to identify with the workers and I suspect that he supports industrial disputes for the same reason. I get the feeling that if he woke up one morning and discovered he was the son of a miner or a railwayman, instead of Lord Stansgate, he would be highly delighted.

Benn's antics through that spring and summer of 1981 inflicted enormous damage on the Labour Party. We suffered heavy losses of votes in a number of parliamentary by-elections as a consequence, nearly losing the rock-solid Labour seat of Warrington to Roy Jenkins of the Social Democrats. Benn gave a great boost to the hard Left as it renewed its efforts to infiltrate the party.

That was the year of the deepest crisis in the party's history. We had experienced divisions and disagreements in the past, but at least we were never afraid to bring them out into the open and fight them publicly. I can still remember the rows we had in the 1950s over German rearmament, Clause Four of the constitution on nationalization, and unilateral nuclear disarmament. Yet profound as those difficulties were, the Labour Party remained basically intact, both organizationally and in terms of an underlying consensus about aims and objectives. In the final analysis, the ability to overcome those problems was proved by our success through the ballot box. Through it all, Labour was able to retain and build victory on the loyalty and support of the electorate.

I was worried in September 1981 that the new crisis placed a major question-mark over each and every one of those facets of the party's existence. Moreover, the party was literally on the verge of bankruptcy. For years it had staggered from deficit to deficit, from overdraft to overdraft. Year after year the National Executive

Committee had come to the unions cap in hand to save them, but now the unions had their own troubles to cope with, as the slump brought falling memberships and tighter finances. Our willingness to help the party was being stretched almost to breaking point.

With only sixty full-time agents in the country for more than 600 constituencies, Labour's organization was in an equally disastrous state. The old official figure for individual membership of 600,000 odd was grossly inflated, based on a quota of 1,000 members per constituency. The true figure was lower than 350,000 and perhaps less than 200,000.

I was conscious as well that Labour was no longer making much of an appeal to the voters. In the May 1979 general election the party's percentage share of the poll was the lowest it had been since the débâcle of August 1931, while in terms of actual numbers voting Labour it was the worst result since 1935 – with the exception of October 1974 when it was 40,000 less on a lower turnout (and in 1983 it was to be even worse).

The truth was staring us in the face in the autumn of 1981: there was no longer that wide measure of loyalty and support for Labour in the electorate that we had been able to count on through thick and thin in the past. We ignored that at our peril.

What has enabled Labour to survive crises in the past has been that the party still retained an underlying consensus about its aims, united in believing that the only way to achieve Socialism was through the ballot box. In September 1981 it seemed to me those days might be numbered. The party had changed with the arrival of the hard Left and groups such as the Militant Tendency in its midst. As far as they are concerned Labour is just a temporary staging post on the way to revolution in the streets.

The Labour Party cannot compromise with intolerance and fanaticism. It has a duty as well as a right to protect itself from those who seek to destroy it. That is why the NUR was in the forefront of those who wanted resolute action taken to deal with the hard-Left threat. Only if this is eradicated can we restore common sense and a genuine spirit of tolerance in the party.

But I also believe that Labour should stand for justice and equality, which lie at the heart of the commitment of my Socialist faith. We continue to live in a society which has failed to solve the age-old evils of poverty and injustice. The return of mass unemployment made it all the more vital that Labour should renew its

141

sense of idealism through a radical progamme of social and economic reform.

I believe that the link between the party and the trade unions remains Labour's greatest strength and we must not allow our weaknesses to destroy that binding tie. It was the breakdown of the partnership between the industrial and political wings of the movement that lost the party the May 1979 general election.

At the 1981 party conference the hard Left suffered some real setbacks. Over the following two years we managed to regain some of the lost ground, but it was a never-ending struggle that dissipated the party's energies from opposition to Mrs Thatcher's Government.

In my 1982 political report I was in a pessimistic mood about the party's future: 'The prospects of a Labour victory in the next general election have never seemed so remote and they will stay remote as long as the present state of civil war within the party persists.' In my view, Labour has to come to terms with the needs of Britain's voters in the last quarter of the twentieth century. 'That is unlikely to mean the hair-shirt socialism of some of our more aristocratic Labour messiahs,' I wrote. 'That kind of fundamentalism is increasingly irrelevant to an electorate which in its majority is still enjoying the benefits of the affluent society, however rapidly these are being eroded by the policies of the present Government.'

At the September 1982 Labour Party conference we made further gains in the National Executive Committee elections, and at last we grasped the nettle of the Militant Tendency. By a massive majority, Conference voted to introduce a new register to cover affiliated organizations to the party, and it was made clear that the Militant Tendency would not be tolerated any longer. There followed months of delay and prevarication, mainly because the leaders of Militant threatened to use the bourgeois courts they were supposed to despise to oppose the party leadership's efforts to deal with them.

In February 1983 the National Executive Committee finally voted to expel the board of the *Militant* newspaper from the Labour Party – but this can only be the start. If Labour is seriously intending to remove the rag, tag and bobtail Trotskyite groups from within the party, the party's Executive Committee will eventually have to take up the issue of the proscribed list as the NUR was already urging in 1980.

Without such vigorous action, Labour will never again have any credibility with the electorate. And if Labour fails, it is not just the party's survival that is at stake but the jobs and standards of life of so many working people whose only hope lies in the success of the Labour movement.

The Struggle for Power in the Union

My stormy years as General Secretary brought an increasingly bitter struggle for power inside the union. The hard Left grew to be a formidable force on the twenty-six-strong Executive Committee, and through a campaign of intimidation and harassment they made life very difficult for all the full-time senior officers working at Unity House. I often felt that I was fighting the battle against them with very little help. What I now regret more than anything else is that I did not do enough to rally people in the union to combat their influence.

It has become a perpetual problem in today's trade unions that the vast majority of the members imply will not get off their backsides and ensure that their union is run in their interests rather than merely for political purposes. In the old days the rank and file used to take a much greater interest in the affairs of their union. The local branches were centres of social life, and used to meet in working-class clubs and pubs. But now most workers believe they have better ways of spending their spare time than sitting up all evening at meetings, which as a result tend to attract only political extremists and bureaucrats. As a result of this apathy, a mere handful can come to gain control of union branches and manipulate them.

It is not only the Left that will try to manipulate the union. In 1980 we learned that the National Front had set up a Railwaymen's Association with the declared objective of fighting the policies and aims of all three rail unions. Regular newsletters filled with racialist propaganda and distortions of our programme were

144

being sent out to members in an attempt to incite them to move against the leadership.

Our rules already gave us power to put a stop to these provocative activities. I warned that any members of the union using their position to further racialist policies would be reported to the Executive. Each case would be examined on its merits and those concerned would receive a fair hearing, with appeal machinery available, but if the accused failed to satisfy the Executive, they would lose their membership card. We were not prepared to have the traditions of our union crushed by a gang of racialists, deliberately infiltrating the union and sowing division, dissension and hatred among the rank and file.

Not long before this outbreak of racialist activity inside the union I had visited Buchenwald concentration camp in Germany. I saw the gas chambers, the ovens where bodies were burned, and the indescribably horrible conditions in which the victims of Nazi persecution lived out their miserable last days. Millions had been Jews, but the earlier sufferers of torture and death were all kinds of people who had stood in the way of Hitler's march to totalitarian insanity, including thousands whose only offence was to be trade unionists.

I believed that the National Front had to be stopped in its tracks before it did any more damage to the union. That is why we took such drastic action, and it succeeded, for the Fascist threat evaporated and we have so far had no further trouble from the lunatic Right.

There was no division of opinion on the union's Executive Committee on that issue, but the hard Left adopted double standards. They were ready to use the rulebook to throw Right-wing extremists out of the NUR, but they took a far more tolerant view of the activities of the extreme Left in the union. It was from that quarter that most of the disruption came during my term of office.

Following the growing infiltration of the Left into the branches, James Knapp became General Secretary after me in March 1983. Only after his election did it become clear how far the hard Left influence had gone. It was as if I had been holding back a political avalanche.

Nevertheless, I do not believe for one moment that the hard Left who dominate some sections of the union organization and who had made Knapp's election possible truly reflect the views of the 150,000 members in the depots, workshops and stations across the

145

country. In my eight years at the top I felt that I had my finger more accurately on the pulse of the rank and file. Certainly they never let me down in a crisis. But, as Edmund Burke said, 'For the triumph of evil it is only necessary that good men do nothing.'

How did the hard Left come to exercise such power in the union? The NUR has always been a highly political union and there is no harm at all in passionate debate and argument. I was never against working with Communists and other Left-wingers, provided that they had the interests of the members at heart. Indeed, the former Communist Dave Bowman was the best President of the union that I had to deal with during my period as General Secretary. He always put the members and the NUR before any political dogma, and I found him a powerful ally once we had reached an agreement. He would always honour undertakings and work for the unity of the union.

Bowman was from an older school of industrial militancy, which has a tradition going back to the beginning of the century. But in recent years a different kind of Left has come into prominence, whose aim is to destroy the unity of the union and try to lead the members by the nose into unrealistic political adventures.

The real trouble lay in the twenty-six-strong full-time Executive Committee. From my early days as General Secretary I had to face a small hard-Left core on that body, but until 1979 they never numbered more than nine, and although they could be an irritant, they lacked an overall majority. But in 1980 the balance started to change and by 1982 the hard Left controlled at least twelve seats, and there were usually a few more supporters they could count on if they put on the pressure.

The hard Left on my Executive Committee even refused to pursue the policy decisions of the union's annual conference. In 1982, for example, the delegates at Plymouth voted overwhelmingly for a motion to consult 'our Socialist comrades in Europe' before any 'final decision' was made about the withdrawal of Britain from the Common Market. The motion also cautioned that a Labour Government should satisfy itself as well as fellow Socialists in the EEC that a decision to pull out would 'not have a disastrous effect upon the economic life of Britain and other members of the EEC'. But the Executive refused to let me act on this resolution.

Similarly, the hard Left on the Executive would not allow me to implement the defence policy of the NUR, which backed multilateral rather than unilateral nuclear disarmament. I wanted to follow up a motion passed by the conference by submitting it to the Labour party conference but I was stopped from doing so by the majority of the Executive Committee.

They also refused to put forward to the Labour Party Conference an NUR conference decision on economic policy. Yet all these three issues were key policy areas in the Labour manifesto for the 1983 General Election. It was during the latter part of Alun Rees's Presidency, which ran from 1978 to 1980, that the Executive Committee got completely out of hand and Rees was unable to do anything about it. They used to demand meetings at the drop of a hat and would then attempt to browbeat the chief officers. But the senior officials have rights as well as the Executive Committee, and the union's constitution is supposed to protect Head Office from intimidation.

Much of the trouble stems from the fact that members of the Executive Committee work full-time on trade union affairs during their three-year period of office, but often there is not enough genuine union work for them to do. This gives them plenty of time to plot and scheme to gain support for policies they approve and to make life difficult for the chief officers.

When Tommy Ham took over as President in January 1981, I and my three assistants insisted that a code of conduct should be established to govern the relations between the Executive Committee and the chief officers. We wanted to establish a proper procedure to follow so that they were not preoccupied all the time with the disruptive demands of the Left. Ham agreed and the code was presented to the Executive. The hard-Left majority accepted it only after I threatened to report the matter to the annual conference.

Another form of harassment adopted by the hard Left was to try and carpet me for weekend political speeches I made from time to time denouncing Tony Benn and the Trotskyist infiltrators into the Labour Party. I was always careful not to stray away from the NUR's policies as agreed by our annual conference, but this did not stop Executive Committee members from writing to the national newspapers dissociating themselves from what I had said. In doing so they only showed their own ignorance of the union's policies.

I had to take great care not to present them with the sort of opportunity they were waiting for to challenge me successfully. The hard Left used to complain that I manipulated the agenda for

147

meetings and kept sensitive items out of their sight. This was utter nonsense, but I did try to ensure that my immediate colleagues were not pressurized by the Executive Committee.

I was never an autocrat. Running a union like the NUR, it would have been impossible to be so even if I had wanted to. But a successful union requires a sense of internal cohesion and discipline to have any hope of being effective in its work for the members. Some of the hard Left were trying to turn Unity House into a stronghold for their extremist position, and I believed that what they were doing was immensely damaging to the well-being of the rank and file who we were all there to represent to the best of our abilities. The Executive Committee wanted me to be their prisoner, to carry their ideological luggage. This has never been my idea of how an elected trade union leader should behave. The General Secretary is not a glorified errand boy.

Gradually I began to realize that the trouble lay wider than in the Executive Committee. I was certain that the effort I was making to combat the extremists' influence in the Labour Party made them decide to attack the union and work for my downfall.

It is no exaggeration to say that a climate of deep distrust was created in our headquarters. The office was like a sieve. Because I was uncertain about the confidentiality of the mail, I made arrangements with my assistants to have important letters posted direct to their home addresses.

There was one very nasty incident in my final year as General Secretary which illustrates the mood of intolerance in head office which infected the Executive Committee, and shows how the hard Left operate when they cannot get their own way. On 7 June 1982 I had called a meeting of my chief officers to discuss the Shildon engineering works and the other threatened works, which had just been temporarily reprieved by the Board. I also invited the chairman and secretary of the Executive's negotiating committee, John Milligan and John Cogger, to come along.

Within a short time a furious row developed and Milligan started threatening me. Suddenly he leaped on to the top of my desk and towered over me. I was sitting in my chair and leaned back to avoid him. As I did so the chair tipped over and I fell flat on my back. Looking up from the floor I saw Milligan still coming over the desk towards me, but my two assistants dragged him back struggling and kicking. Tommy Ham went quite white and I thought he was going to faint. I was lucky not to have been injured

Afterwards I took legal advice about the incident. Our solicitors sent Milligan a letter warning him that if anything like that happened again I would take legal proceedings against him.

I first became aware of the subversive organizations working inside the union during the summer of 1981, when they launched a campaign of lies against our policies and leadership. During our fortnight's stay in St Andrews for our annual conference a group from the Marxist Militant Tendency operated out of the university, and they put the heat on the delegates with leafleting and fringe meetings. The Militants and their allies were campaigning for Benn in his election battle against Denis Healey for the Labour deputy leadership, but they also wanted to influence policy issues on our agenda including unilateral nuclear disarmament, the Common Market and action to deal with groups such as theirs.

The Militants also produced a pamphlet published by the Cambridge Heath Press at Mentmore Terrace in London E8, publishers of the *Militant* newspaper. Entitled *A Fighting Programme for the NUR*, it was a blatant interference in the internal affairs of the union. The document pushed not only for an aggressive policy of strikes on the railways but also for changes in our rules to make the NUR what they called 'a fighting Socialist union'. The Militants proposed the re-election of officials at the branches every three years; every branch to have a delegate at the annual conference; powers to be given to district councils to call strikes; and a drastic change in the machinery of negotiation which would give greater control to the union representatives in the local departmental committees, who would be recallable by the branches at any time.

During 1981 I received from branches a growing dossier of documentary evidence that the hard Left was moving into the union in a big way. In June 1981 an NUR Broad Left organization was established, with a powerful role played by the Militant Tendency. Members of the Executive Committee as well as activists from union branches and local departmental committees took part. In the first edition of its journal, *Left Lines*, the Broad Left called on 'the power of the NUR, along with all other railworkers, together with the Triple Alliance and with the broader Labour movement' to drive what it called 'this anti-working class government' from office and press for the return of Labour pledged to 'a socialist plan of production'. The implication of this call was clearly that the NUR should use its industrial muscle to force political change.

At a meeting of the Bennite Labour Co-ordinating Committee in July 1981 at the Central Hall, Westminster, Ian Williams – a member of the Executive – actually boasted to the delegates that a Broad Left organization had been set up inside the union a few weeks earlier.

Trotskyists from outside the NUR felt free to meddle in our affairs. Peter Taaffe, the editor of *Militant* and recently expelled from the Labour Party, actually sent out a circular to the union's branches and district councils. He urged that 'resolutions, telegrams and letters of protest' should be sent to the union's Executive to 'make clear' that there was 'opposition to any bans, proscriptions, witch-hunts and attempts to restrict political discussion in the Labour movement'.

Taaffe even suggested that Militant speakers should be invited to NUR branch meetings so that the group could explain their policies and programmes. 'No amount of undemocratic manoeuvring by the Right-wing will prevent the growth of Militant's ideas and influence,' he ended his circular. 'However, NUR members can now play a major role in defeating this latest Right-wing attack and be in the forefront of the campaign for a clear socialist alternative.'

Militant organized a petition inside the union against 'witch-hunts'. A special bulletin from the *Militant* suggested that I had delivered 'vicious and distorted personal attacks' on 'genuine Socialists who work hard for the party', while sitting on platforms with leading politicians like Shirley Williams and Bill Rodgers, who had then gone off to form the SDP. The broadsheet further suggested that branches should not merely invite Militant speakers along to talk to them, but also donate money to the Militant fighting fund and sell the newspaper.

More than fifty branches of the union sent me complaints about the subversive activities of Militant and their hangers-on. Branch officials were especially concerned that much of the literature was being sent to them personally by full-time organizers of the Tendency, although names and addresses of branch secretaries are supposed to be confidential.

A well-known full-time Militant organizer who was not a railwayman, Martin Elvin, was known to have been actively pressing the organization's campaign at the NUR conference in St Andrews. It was also reported to me that he had turned up at a meeting of the Feltham Number One branch of the union uninvited and asked to speak on behalf of Militant, but he was told to leave. He was got rid of only with some difficulty, finally departing when the branch resolved unanimously to kick him out. Several other branch secretaries complained to me about having Militant representatives accosting them on their doorsteps, demanding they should be entitled to go along to NUR meetings and address the members.

Other subversive organizations were also moving into the union in 1981. The Socialist Workers' Party, a Trotskyist group outside the Labour Party, set up what they called a 'rank-and-file' organization, which published a broadsheet calling for strike action. 'Resolutions through branches are not enough. We have to begin by taking unofficial action at the bottom,' it declared. 'We have to get our local departmental committees to call mass meetings so that what is really at stake can be discussed.' One paragraph in the paper called for the building of a rank-and-file organization to challenge and defeat the NUR's leadership. 'Our leadership,' it said, 'need to be no more than delegates, paid by us, accountable to us, and told by us what to do.' That paper was sent out to the branches with a covering letter from one Brian Maddock, an NUR member of Sussex Terrace, Brighton.

When I found out what was going on in some of the branches I sent out a special circular to them on 5 June 1981, pointing out these publications were in breach of the rules of the union. It states clearly in Rule 10 in the NUR rulebook that: 'No officer, member, branch, district council or national grades conference shall issue any circular relating to the union in general (except it be a proposal to alter the Rules) unless such circular is sanctioned by the Executive Committee or the General Secretary in writing.' I told the branches to ignore the subversive material being pushed round the union and made it clear that none of the literature should be discussed at branch or district council meetings. I also warned that union funds should not be used to help those unofficial bodies.

Then the Plymouth district council passed a resolution for the attention of the Executive Committee asking for the circulation of Militant propaganda inside the union to be stopped and action taken against NUR members involved in its distribution. No less than seven of the twenty-six district councils, as well as around fifty branches, backed those demands. I put all their resolutions together with a full report on the evidence we had received before the Executive Committee, along with the accusations made against named individuals who had been involved in subversive activity.

One of the leading culprits was a member of the Executive, Ian Williams, who had only joined the union in 1973. His name appeared on a broadsheet in which he was billed to address the inaugural meeting of the NUR Broad Left on 6 June 1981, which was dedicated to attacks on the policies of the union. Williams also made disclosures to the press about correspondence he had with me, though this was also against the rules of the union.

Another was Geoffrey Hensby, secretary of Paddington Number One branch. He claimed it was not his intention to break the union rules by circulating leaflets. Hensby was a hard-Left candidate in the 1983 election for my successor as General Secretary, and he is an active member of the Broad Left group. As an officer in the union he was in clear breach of the rules.

Then there was Mr T. Doyle of the Tinsley branch of the NUR, who joined the union in 1972. Like the others he claimed he was speaking 'in a personal capacity' when he addressed the Broad Left conference. But he wrote to me saying that he did not know he was breaking the rules of the union by his behaviour. The others involved were B. Maddock of Brighton, already mentioned, and G. Cantwell from Perth.

The union's Executive decided to refer the whole question to a special sub-committee for examination, but the hard Left ensured that this body was packed with their own people. They were continually looking for excuses to do nothing at all with the dossier of evidence about subversion in the union. We went on for weeks but the volume of material forced even this unbalanced committee to accept that they would be failing in their responsibility within the NUR's own rules if they did not condemn interference in our internal affairs.

The special committee 'in particular' deplored the way in which outside bodies had resorted to 'distortions of the truth' about the activities of the Executive Committee and of myself. They suggested that I should send out another circular to the branches, warning them that branch meetings were occasions for discussions of the union's affairs, not for the activities of unofficial organizations. The committee's report went on to suggest that while nobody had any wish to stop members from reading what they wanted, the NUR's constitution should not be abused by 'providing a free platform for bodies which had no standing within the union, but which seek to bring undue influence to bear on the membership and the branches on matters which have been determined by the union's governing bodies'.

The report also found that Williams was guilty of breaching union rules, as were Hensby and Doyle. We showed remarkable tolerance of what had been happening by deciding not to apply the provisions of the rule and fine them, but merely to ask for assurances that they would obey the rules and constitution of the union in future.

Even so, five members of the sub-committee would not go as far as to reprimand the people concerned. They couldn't deny that the rules had been broken, but they suggested that the rules had been 'applied in a manner that [could be construed as] restricting . . . the political rights' of members.

Tommy Ham, the President, ruled out that argument on the grounds that there had been a breach of the union's rules and he could not therefore accept any suggestion to the contrary. But when the full Executive Committee debated the matter, the hard Left and their allies rejected all the findings of the special committee by 17 votes to 7.

The decision placed Tommy Ham and myself in an awkward position because it implied we should turn a blind eye to breaches of the rules.

I was outraged by the position I was now in and thought it proper to obtain legal advice on the situation which had now arisen with a view to protecting the union's interests.

The advice confirmed the sub-committee's findings that the documents sent out by Militant were circulars, and as they had been distributed without the consent of the Executive Committee or General Secretary there was a breach of rule. I was also told that the Executive had a duty to ensure that the rules were upheld and that the Executive itself was a creature of the rules and subject to them.

It was clear therefore the Executive were putting the union in a situation where an aggrieved member or branch would have a good chance of successfully challenging their decision before a court on the basis that they were in breach of rule.

I then issued a circular to the branches informing them of the Executive Committee's failure to take any action on the sub-committee's report, and many reacted immediately and angrily.

153

Despite having received legal advice that I should now submit the matter to the Executive again for their reconsideration I decided that the proper place to which it should be referred was the annual conference, even though I was aware that the Executive would use every trick to stop it being debated there.

While the issue was awaiting debate at the 1982 annual conference, the hard Left took no notice of the complaints and continued to burrow away inside the union with impunity. During the early months of 1982 they tried to stir up opposition among our guards to flexible rostering, in alliance with ASLEF. A bulletin issued in February, said to be on behalf of the 'rank-and-file railworkers' and published from a box number at 73 Walmgate in York, argued that train guards were 'threatening a national one-day unofficial strike' over the flexible rostering issue. It suggested they 'would try to reconvene the union's annual general meeting in an attempt to change its constitution and oust the General Secretary Sidney Weighell'. More than eighty NUR members were said to have met unofficially in London to examine ways of pursuing their campaign. They claimed to represent 1,700 guards.

Mike Burgess, a spokesman for the guards' steering committee, is reported to have said: 'We most certainly want to see Sid Weighell out. He is treating us like little boys. Our action is as much against Mr Weighell as British Rail.' He went on to say that they wanted to replace me with 'a General Secretary and an Executive answerable and truly representing the people who pay their wages'.

Leaflets of this kind were being circulated around the branches in a deliberate attempt to stir up discontent, and as a result guards from twenty-five London depots voted for an unofficial stoppage on 19 February in protest at our acceptance of flexible rostering. Unbelievably, the meeting was addressed by Ian Williams, who as an Executive member was bound by the decision to go along with flexible rostering for the guards. He said that he spoke 'in a personal capacity' and told them he was the only member of the Executive who had voted against the issue.

I was in no doubt that extremist elements were trying to push our members into senseless disruption. I sent out a circular to all the depots warning the rank and file that those who had voted for a 'day of action' over flexible rostering on 19 February were 'just out to destroy the railway industry'.

An unofficial bulletin from the Militant-dominated Brighton

branch openly admitted what they were trying to do: 'the one-day strike is part of an all-out campaign to get the flexible rostering agreement torn up. At the moment the campaign only involves guards, as they are going to be most severely and immediately affected by the deal. But as the going gets harder financially for British Railways Board, they will be seeking even greater flexibility for more and more workers in an effort to cut the wage bill. The guards hope that other grades will come to see the relevance for them of their campaign and give it their support.'

A leaflet published by the Socialist Workers' Party from 265 Seven Sisters Road, London N4 advocated joint ASLEF-NUR action in picketing and striking, while another from the so-called Rail Workers' Fraction of the Rank and File openly urged members to 'set up cells of rank and file in your union, work for a national strike to smash Thatcher and kick out Right-wing union leaders who compromise with the bosses'. The leaflet was so extreme that it even called for support for the killers within the IRA and INLA whom it called 'freedom fighters'.

The idiot Left were now crawling out from under the stones and exploiting the rail crisis, and hard-Left members of the Executive Committee did not seem to give a damn about what was happening. Yet the agreement which was being attacked was one endorsed by an Executive decision. In fact, during the stoppage of 1982 the hard Left on the Executive were in constant contact with ASLEF headquarters. One morning I was astonished to see a photograph on the front page of the *Morning Star*, which showed Jock Nicholson, a prominent Communist Party member on the Executive, together with other members of the union's Executive Committee handing over a £100 cheque to support the ASLEF leaders, with the NUM's Communist Vice-President Mick McGahey looking on. There was also a piece in the *Sun* on the incident. I played hell about that at a meeting of the full Executive Committee, for it was quite contrary to the union's policy.

During this period in the flexible rostering disputes, I found it necessary to obtain police protection on a number of occasions when going to meetings. I began to take the precaution of never standing near the edge of the station platform when travelling on the London Underground.

I had become a real thorn in the flesh of the hard Left. It appeared that I had replaced the EETPU leader Frank Chapple as their Enemy Number One. The Brighton branch of the union was a particular centre of idiocy and it put down a motion to our annual conference, expressing no confidence in my leadership, with particular reference to flexible rostering. In the event, Brighton could not find a seconder for the motion and it was not debated.

As I had anticipated, many branches and district councils demanded that the Militant Tendency's activities be placed before the Plymouth conference. I told the delegates that it was a 'blatant insult' to their intelligence to suggest they were conducting a witch-hunt by examining what had been going on inside the union. They were the custodians of the constitution and it was up to them to protect it from abuse. In a three-hour debate many of the delegates spoke out against the Executive Committee's failure to deal with the subversives: 'They have received notices, letters verbal say-so, that they will not do it again but they are like slugs, they go underground until it rains again and then they come out and eat slowly away into the heart and soul of the union,' said one delegate.

One of them was so angry with an article in *Tribune* by Williams attacking the NUR that he suggested he should be expelled from the union, and he was applauded for saying so. 'I would just say to Williams that you do not go into the tiger's cage and bite its tail because it is going to bloody well bite back,' he said. Another suggested expulsion for the people responsible unless they gave written assurances to their union branches that they would not distribute subversive material again. By 54 votes to 23 the delegates overturned the Executive Committee's verdict, and the individuals named in the report were each fined £10 and given a warning not to break the rules again.

The hard Left also made efforts to drastically change the rules of the union at the 1982 conference, specifically in that the General Secretary should be subject to re-election by the members every five years. Opposing this, I said: 'The power in this union resides with you and the Executive Committee and the officers carry out the decisions you make to the letter. I have to stand up and argue for policies that I opposed many a time. If you carry this, the General Secretary will spend about four years between the five-year elections going around promising the world to everybody, buying votes by telling them anything in order to gain votes. Do you say that is democracy? It is absolute rubbish and you know it.'

I know that re-election of full-time officials in the union would make the organization less efficient, and it would not provide the qualified men needed for the complex work. Those pressing for the change did not want a proper General Secretary of the union, but a tame pigeon whose neck they could wring if it suited them to.

It was quite clear from the decisive defeat of the hard Left at the Plymouth conference that many delegates were in the mood to take drastic action to drive the extremists out of the union, and were ready to quash subversion. In retrospect, I regret that I did not inform the conference of the strong legal advice I had received about the behaviour of the seventeen Executive Committee members who had chosen to disregard the rules of the union in dealing with the subversive threat. Too leniently, I held back from doing so. It was a mistake, a sign of weakness, and I have lived to regret it. The 1982 Plymouth conference seemed ready to give me the support I needed to clean up the union and rout the hard Left. I thought the rebuke delivered by the delegates to the Executive Committee would be enough to bring some sanity back into the union. But I was wrong.

The Road to Birmingham

The battles inside the union culminated in the events at the Labour Party conference in 1982 which led to my resignation. But I am sure I did the right thing at the conference, and I would do the same again if necessary. My decision not to cast the union's block vote for the NUM candidate Eric Clarke in the party's National Executive Committee elections was demanded by the best interests of the Labour movement, and in my view was in accord with the wishes of the delegates at the 1982 annual conference.

The background was that various union leaders were worried that Labour did not stand a chance of winning the next general election unless something was done about the extremists. We began working together in 1981 to change the balance of power on the party Executive so that more sensible voices might prevail. We wanted to ensure that action was taken to deal with the Militant Tendency who were wrecking Labour in the eyes of the voters, and then to create the potential to defeat the Tories.

Good progress was made at the conference that year. Eric Varley beat Norman Atkinson for the party treasurership, while Shirley Summerskill, Betty Boothroyd and Gwyneth Dunwoody won seats in the women's section. We also managed to defeat Benn's bid for the deputy leadership, although that was a near thing. In fact, it was his bad luck that NUPE, normally controlled by the Left, decided to find whom its members wanted as deputy leader and got the wrong answer when the rank and file backed Denis Healey. If that had not happened, Benn would have won easily.

In 1982 we decided to press further in getting moderates on to the National Executive. But I knew that the NUR Executive would want to support the Left-wing slate for the elections. There was one way of taking control of the decision from the Executive, which was to ask the annual conference to make that decision. The Bristol branch of the union, which was concerned at what was taking place in the party, sent a motion in to Conference which said that we should vote for the same twelve trade union nominees as we had supported in 1981.

Now, you have to do a lot of horse-trading in the elections for the Labour Party National Executive, but everybody does it – both on the Left and on the Right. In fact, it was the better organization of the trade union block votes on the Left over the past ten years or so that had ensured their control of the Executive.

For that reason we were never certain that our man, Assistant General Secretary Russell Tuck, would be voted on to the Executive each year in the trade union section, even though we could usually count on his getting far more votes than he needed to get elected. However, it had been my canvassing for support at previous party conferences that had ensured Bob Kettle, a leading Left-winger in the NUR, a seat on Labour's standing orders committee – although he seemed to forget this when he later condemned my actions at Blackpool.

When the Bristol branch motion came up for debate at the Plymouth conference I made clear to the delegates the only basis on which I could support the resolution. It is normal practice for the General Secretary to put a motion into context and explain on what understanding it is acceptable. As the verbatim account of that discussion says: 'This governing body is going to decide and all they have said is what the Executive Committee did last year was right and proper [in the votes cast in the Labour Executive elections] so do it again this year. That is what they are saying and they are saying more, that we have got a nice, sensible, balanced party Executive Committee which will lead us into the next general election in some sort of unified form.' But I also reminded delegates that I had to trade for votes in the party conference. 'That is the world you and I live in,' I argued. It was on that understanding that delegates carried the Bristol resolution.

The NUR had voted for Eric Clarke, the NUM candidate for Labour's Executive, in previous years in return for the Mineworkers voting for our man Russell Tuck. I had had a good relationship with Joe Gormley when he was the NUM President, but in April 1982 he retired and Arthur Scargill took over. With Joe I had been able to keep in close contact and I could rely on him to deliver his side of any bargain but with Scargill it was a different kettle of fish. I had already had dealings with Scargill over the NUR strike in July 1982, and I realized I was not working with a man of the quality of Joe Gormley.

So on 3 September I wrote a letter to the NUM General Secretary Lawrence Daly asking him whether his union would be voting for our man in the party National Executive elections at the Labour conference, in return for us voting for their candidate Eric Clarke. It was this seat on the party Executive I was concerned with. Backing the Mineworkers' nominees for the treasurership and the conference arrangements committee was not the same because their election did not affect the NUR seat on the Executive in the trade union section.

If either Scargill or Daly had written back and said 'yes' to my written request I would have cast our block vote in favour of Clarke in line with the Plymouth conference decision. But I never received any reply to my letter and no contact was made with me or my office. If the NUM leaders were anxious to secure the votes for Clarke they should have got in touch with me. I waited until the last minute in Blackpool before casting the NUR vote.

As a result I voted in accordance with the conference decision for 11 out of the 12 trade union section nominees they had chosen, but I used the twelfth vote in accordance with my interpretation of what we had decided at Plymouth. This meant that I voted for Tom Breakell of the EETPU because Frank Chapple, the Electricians' leader, had guaranteed his union's 270,000 votes for Russell Tuck. The sole object was to secure the seat for the NUR man.

In the normal course of events I would have reported this to my own Executive Committee at their December meeting after they received a full written report of the proceedings of the Labour Party conference. I expect there would have been a bit of a domestic storm, but any fair-minded Executive member on examining the detailed notes of the 1982 NUR conference debate on the issue would have reached no other conclusion than that I had acted in the best interests of the union and the party. In fact, any Executive Committee of a few years ago would have agreed in five minutes flat that I had done right.

However, a whole chapter of incidents at Blackpool changed the position. First of all, it was discovered that the trade union section votes had been counted wrongly by the tellers, and the National Executive ballot on the trade union section had to be added up again. Then, contrary to the rules, somebody showed the votes cast in favour of Clarke, who had failed to hold his seat, to certain union leaders, and it was soon round the conference hall that the NUR had not voted for him.

The hard Left were already furious that the balance of the National Executive had been changed to dramatically, with a further gain of four seats for the moderates. All hell broke out and I was surrounded by people eager to bring me down. There were many Left-wingers on our conference delegation who wanted to use the incident against me. Back in London certain Executive Committee members convened an unofficial meeting and by a majority decided that I should be suspended from office, without waiting for an explanation.

On Friday morning we travelled south from Blackpool. I usually sit in the front of the car with the union's driver Len because my wife likes to smoke and I don't. But on this occasion I sat in the back of the Ford Granada because I wanted to think out what I should do and decide my next move.

By the time we had stopped for lunch at a pub just off junction 13 on the M1 I had made up my mind to resign. I was battle-weary by that stage and getting a little sick of the endless scheming. Half of me relished the challenge of the struggle, but the other half yearned to get a fishing rod and head off for a trout stream. I had already decided anyway to leave around October 1983 and Joan and I had been up to the Harrogate area to look for a house.

But there was another important issue. I hoped to get the union's recall conference, due to meet in Birmingham a fortnight later, to accept the 6 per cent McCarthy Tribunal award. I believed my presence at the meeting to be crucial to save the union from a disastrous rerun of the summer conflict. Under the rules, if I resigned I could not be suspended by the Executive, and so would remain in office throughout the three months' notice period.

If I had been suspended, I would not even have been able to attend the conference at all. The Executive would have kept me hanging on a nail at the back of the door while the union took the important decision on the McCarthy award, and if the delegates rejected the award it would have created chaos both inside the union and throughout the railway industry.

I told Joan over Sunday lunch at our home in Bishop's Stortford what I had decided to do and she agreed with me. She was also getting weary of the constant battles raging inside the union over the past few years, a sad change from the more agreeable times in my first five years as General Secretary.

I decided to let my senior officers know what I was planning. I did not want any press leaks or publicity, so I arranged to meet them two days later, on the evening of Tuesday 5 October, at the Red Lion Hotel in Radlett. We all travelled there separately and by different routes. When I explained my decision to them they tried to persuade me to change my mind, but I told them that to go before the Executive Committee was like appearing before a kangaroo court, because they had already decided to suspend me without giving me any opportunity to explain my side of the story.

I suggested that if they had any better ideas on what to do I should like to hear them. It was argued that I might be ready to rethink my decision to resign if there was evidence of a genuine groundswell of support for me in the union among the rank and file. But I did not want to be involved in any such ploy.

The next day I walked into the boardroom at Unity House to meet the Executive Committee. Tommy Ham, who had been at the private meeting the night before, told them I had an announcement to make. I then read out my letter of resignation as General Secretary: 'In casting the union's vote in the party Executive elections I was of course acutely aware of the resolution of the annual conference which had been adopted by the NUR Executive. However, it was, in my view, a fundamental factor in the annual conference's resolution that our candidate would have the support of those unions whose candidates we in turn intended to support. I believe that is quite clear from the transcript of the debate at the annual conference.'

I told the Executive I had waited 'until the last possible moment on the day of voting' for a response from the NUM leaders to my letter of September 3 asking for support for Russell Tuck in return for our backing for Eric Clarke. No response had come, even at the last minute. 'As a matter of personal judgement I then concluded that our union could not count upon that vote,' I said in my statement. 'Being in this very difficult situation I decided that I should adopt the course of action which would best protect the seat of our candidate. I decided not to vote for the Mineworkers' candidate and advised the President accordingly. I, of course, accept full responsibility for that decision.'

Then I went on to acknowledge that I was 'fully aware of the strength of the arguments which can and will be mounted against my interpretation of how the union's vote should have been cast in these circumstances and that this difficult constitutional issue will generate a considerable amount of heated debate at all levels within the union.

'But whatever the constitutional niceties I want it to be firmly understood that my interpretation was reached in the best interests of the union and in an attempt to apply the intention behind the annual conference resolution to a situation which was never anticipated when that resolution was debated and carried.'

And I went on: 'I am, however, continually mindful that the enormous problems facing the railway industry at the present time will test the union to its limits. This is not the time to subject the membership to long and controversial arguments on the union's rules and constitution. Over the next few months decisions will have to be taken by this union which will have a profound effect on our entire membership and indeed on the whole railway industry. The General Secretary of the NUR is the chief spokesman of the union and it is he that bears the responsibility for advancing the policies of the union as laid down by the annual conference. These are policies in which I passionately believe.'

I ended by saying: 'The hostile attitude taken by certain elements towards me in recent months is such that I feel that many of the union's policies will be prejudiced by my seeking to advance them. I have therefore decided that the time has come for another person to take on this difficult but crucial role. Throughout my union career I have always considered the future of the union and its members to be paramount and I will not deviate from this principle now.' So under Rule 5 clause 12 I resigned as General Secretary. I went on to argue that I believed I had acted in the best interests of the union, and according to the spirit of the Plymouth resolution. Then I handed my note of resignation to Tommy Ham and walked out of the room.

There was a look of complete shock on the faces of the hard Left on the Executive, who had not anticipated what I was going to do. After I left they passed a resolution accepting my resignation. That meant I stayed on as General Secretary until 5 January 1983. In accordance with the union's rules my departure put an end to the issue.

However, several hours later, the hard-Left members of the

Executive began to realize that I would be able to go to the Birmingham conference on 13 and 14 October and deal with the controversial McCarthy award. They tried repeatedly over the next few days to persuade Tommy Ham to force me to convene a special meeting of the Executive to reconsider the matter. They would dearly have liked to suspend me despite my resignation so as to stop me speaking for the McCarthy award at the special conference.

I stayed away from my office, but I did have a long-standing engagement up in York on 9 October. I found I still had a lot of support in the north, and the meeting of NUR members at the Station Hotel gave me an overwhelming vote of confidence. Letters were pouring into Head Office, demanding that I should reconsider my decision to resign and let the issue be decided at Birmingham by the delegates. Among the many messages of sympathy over my decision to resign, I had a number from senior figures in the party.

Every one of the 550 branches of the union was sent details of the events at Blackpool and a copy of my resignation statement, together with the verbatim report of the debate at Plymouth on the way the NUR block vote should be cast at the party Executive elections, so all the members were in a good position to judge the rights and wrongs of the issue. I decided to leave it to the common sense of the delegates at the Birmingham conference to decide whether they really wanted me to withdraw my resignation.

There were highly emotional scenes around the Engineering Workers' hall in Birmingham where the recall conference was held. The hard Left turned up outside in strength from all over the country, and many there were not even NUR members. Even Derek Robinson ('Red Robbo'), the sacked Communist British Leyland senior convenor, and his henchmen were waving placards condemning me. I had to have a police escort to get to and from the meeting hall. The hard Left had been organizing their forces during the days since my resignation. They were determined to dominate the conference and prevent any majority vote asking me to reconsider my decision, and were also scheming for rejection of the McCarthy award.

Many have said that I would have won at Birmingham if I had decided to address the delegates. Perhaps I could have swung enough votes in my direction if I had been there, but I stayed away from the hall for the debate itself. By 41 votes to 36 the conference decided not to ask me to tear up my resignation.

Perhaps I should have done more but I thought it was about time that other people did some work for the cause of common sense. I must admit that I was a little disappointed that the delegates did not want me to reconsider my decision. I could not disguise my disgust with my opponents, particularly when I saw the jubilation of the hard Left at their victory. Yet I also felt relief that the endless struggles were over. The conflict inside the union between the destructive Left on the Executive on one side and myself and the chief officers on the other had grown very bitter.

After the vote against me the place was in turmoil. There were more pressmen and photographers crowded in the nearby Albany Hotel where I was waiting than I have seen in my life, all clamouring for a statement. But I brushed them aside and went into lunch with my senior officers. We sat together in the dining room and I told them that in view of the morning decision of the delegates, one of them would have to argue for the 6 per cent McCarthy pay award in the afternoon. However, none of them was willing to do so and it fell on me to persuade the conference, which had rejected me in the morning, to accept the Tribunal decision.

It was to be my last major act as General Secretary and perhaps one of the most important things I ever did. I had prepared myself well in advance to argue the case for accepting the McCarthy award, and many who listened to what I had to say believe it was one of the best speeches I ever made.

I began by reminding the delegates that we had suspended our strike on 28 June in the honest belief that we had a good case to present to Lord McCarthy and his colleagues. What none of us at that time had known was that ASLEF intended to take further industrial action over flexible rostering. Their July escapades had cost British Rail as much as £240 million in lost revenue, compared with the £16 million loss we had caused by our two days of disruption. McCarthy himself estimated that the money lost was the equivalent of 14 per cent of the total paybill for the railway industry.

I told the delegates: 'By the time I presented the case to the Tribunal the background of the arguments and the basis upon which you decided at Plymouth had changed dramatically, not only from the depressed state of the economy knocking hell out of our industry, but in addition [because] we were struggling to keep our feet after the second wave of devastating industrial action.'

I then went through the 6 per cent award in considerable detail,

165

particularly the sensitive parts dealing with productivity. We could expect to see further improvements in pay flowing from our acceptance of changes such as the open station and flexible rostering, and we were ready to test in experiments the driver-only operation of freight trains as long as tough safety conditions were met by the Board. On the thorny issue of guards on the new electrified route from London St Pancras to Bedford, the McCarthy Tribunal had accepted our point that the guards should be kept on the trains at least for six months but with a new function to protect revenue by looking out for fare dodgers. The next problem I dealt with was the 'trainman' concept, a proposed structure for grade promotions to break down the barriers to promotion in the industry, which would be of special benefit to our guards and generally to the traffic grades in the industry with the introduction of new technologies over the next twenty years.

I told the conference that we could not pick and choose between bits of the McCarthy award. We had to either accept it in its entirety or reject it outright. I warned of the responsibilities on their shoulders in making their decision: 'There are a quarter of a million people out there faced with problems that I know about, where the money comes from for paying the rent or buying a pair of shoes for the kids. The industry will be thrown into further industrial chaos if we reject this and I could not pretend or even guess at the final outcome, except this – the certainty of a small industry and thousands of jobs sacrificed. That is the world you live in, that is the world I live in and that is the reality of life that we face now.'

I argued for accepting the award, tough though it was to do so: 'If anybody tells you they can reject it and do something different or better, let him explain what he proposes in detail. Let him explain how he is going to survive the critical months ahead. I will tell you...if we do not win the next general election I do not know whether there is going to be any industry left for you at all.'

At the end of the ensuing discussion I was called on to sum up. What I said can be seen as a conclusion to my public career as General Secretary.

I warned delegates that if they did not co-operate with the new technologies that would be coming into the railway industry, then the network would surely die. Even a change of Government would not alter these facts of life. The argument was about how to adapt to technological developments, not whether the union should resist them blindly. 'You went to the Tribunal. The decision is there, either to accept or reject, and if you reject you only get to the barricades. Let me tell you this, I do not advocate "To the barricades" every Monday morning like Scargill. I am telling you the situation we face. We have to make cold, hard, realistic calculations of what we are doing in this situation.'

I then turned on those critics who kept saying the members were low-paid: 'Nobody fought harder for this industry and the men than I have. It is an insult to the union to say you are the bottom of the league when you know perfectly well you are not. Do you know there are some people in this industry going home with £250 a week and I am having to fight like hell asking them not to work overtime? If we could eliminate even a small proportion of the overtime I could create 15,000 jobs tomorrow.'

And I ended: 'I will tell you this, if you think you are leading an army which will follow you, all right, make a decision and go on strike. You are not leading men who are lacking in courage but you are leading men with intelligence. If you lead them intelligently, they respond intelligently. If you make stupid, cockeyed decisions, they will abandon you. That is your responsibility.'

The majority of delegates, who had voted against me in the morning, now gave me their support over the McCarthy award. By 42 votes to 34 they turned down a motion to reject the McCarthy award and then voted 44 to 32 to accept it.

But even after they had got rid of me, the extremists still did not give up their vindictive attitude. Joan and I were not invited to the union's Executive Christmas dinner, in defiance of tradition. And despite my long service in the union, I never had one word of thanks from the Executive. When the new headquarters were opened on 3 May 1983 I was not even sent an invitation, although it had been my efforts that had brought about the building of the new Unity House against widespread opposition from both the hard Left and Camden council.

But fortunately there were plenty of others outside the Executive Committee who would have nothing to do with the malicious attitude of those small-minded people. Our twelve NUR MPs gave Joan and me a special presentation lunch in the House of Commons. The North-East region, where I first started off my trade union career, made a point of saying goodbye properly. The Darlington and York district council arranged a special function attended by active NUR members and their wives, and made a presentation which included a personal tribute in verse from Shildon works.

What followed in the election for my successor was not what I had hoped for. But my plans to organize the succession in a rational way, knowing that I would retire soon anyway, were originally knocked on the head because I had been unable to find out when my senior colleagues were also planning to retire. Russell Tuck would not indicate his intentions, and did not make up his mind to retire early until just before I resigned. I was kept fully informed by some officers in Unity House about the election for my job, and I became very alarmed at the hard Left's campaign for James Knapp, an inexperienced younger official who had only been in Head Office for a few months.

I would have preferred Charlie Turnock, one of my Assistant General Secretaries, to have won. He was the most capable and the best by every test that can be applied. But he was attacked by the extreme Left both inside and outside the union, and was branded as unsuitable because of his loyalty to me and the decisions taken by the NUR's chief officers during my eight years as General Secretary. One attack on him in the *New Statesman* actually blamed him for Knapp's failure to pass the examination for Assistant General Secretary in 1981.

I had no hesitation in declaring my interest and preference for Charlie Turnock, not because of any personal feelings but in the best interests of the membership of the union. I had seen all the candidates for my job at work. I knew their abilities, and I can only say that the branches made the wrong choice. With the industry and the union facing great problems, it needed the best and most experienced man to deal with them. It must have come as a great disappointment to Charlie Turnock that he lost.

But the hard Left were better organized in the branches, and Knapp was elected in March 1983. No doubt they are well satisfied with his election, but time will tell the extent to which their feelings of victory are justified. In my opinion, these people want either leaders who share their same warped and intolerant ideas or weak men who are wet behind the ears, individuals they can drag about by the nose.

Yet at the end of the day the ordinary member will have to carry the can in the NUR. That is why I have spent my whole life urging the rank and file to get off their backsides and involve themselves in the branches. Forty years on I still have my father's words ringing in my ears: 'Don't complain to me, do something about it yourself.' And that goes for anybody who grumbles that he is not being consulted and can't get his opinions heard.

I make no apologies for what I did at the 1982 Labour Party conference. I am proud and delighted to have done my bit to bring back a measure of sanity to the Labour National Executive: it gave them a chance to clear the members of Militant out of the party and re-establish the credibility of the Labour movement with the voters before the general election. This is a life-and-death issue for the trade unions, and railway workers have more at stake than most.

The increasingly successful penetration of my own union by the hard Left over my last three years as General Secretary shows the terrible dangers to reason and decency that the extremists pose to the wider Labour movement. I hope that what happened to me will be a lesson others will learn, because if they don't many more unions will face a similar menace in the next few years, which could deliver a death blow to the movement.

Where are We Going?

The June 1983 General Election defeat has left the Labour movement in a state of deep crisis, unsure about where it should go, and
confronting a Government opposed to its views on social justice
and a planned economy. Over the next few years the trade unions
will be tested as they have not been since between the wars.

The party and the trade unions both have their roots in the
Chapel and both were sustained in difficult times by comradeship
and by the united cause to win political and industrial power for
working people. Traditionally their aim has been to build Jeru-
salem in England's 'green and pleasant land'. But this goal has yet
to be achieved – indeed it has even moved much further away. To
reach it the Labour movement must be concerned with the well-
being of *all* the people, and must remember that a movement built
on the sound foundations of freedom and quality is much greater
than any one individual. If we forget this, the movement will
surely die. Tragically, however, too many people in Labour's ranks
today have, indeed, forgotten this fact, or never knew it.

The great Labour party leader Clem Attlee put it well in 1937 in
The Labour Party in Perspective: 'During all my years in the
Movement, what has impressed me most is that its strength
depends, not on the brilliance of individuals, but on the quality of
the rank and file. It is the self-sacrifice, idealism and character of
the men and women who do the everyday work of the Party up and
down the country that make me hopeful of the future. It is not the
theories so much as the lives of those who advocate them which
really count in the progress of a great movement.'

170

Today, especially after its electoral disaster, there is a real danger that the Labour movement will go into a terminal decline, collapsing into squabbling sects. If this happens the consequences will be appalling. As Attlee realized, the Labour movement can only survive and prosper if it wins the hearts and minds of the millions who work in Britain's factories and offices. The aim of all those who care for it should be to turn the unions and the party into far more effective organizations on the lines I have drawn out, so that they can become capable once again of forming a broad mass movement.

This means urgent attention must be given to the policy-making process of the Party. The outdated methods of Party Conference, which produces policies so out of touch with Labour's traditional supporters that they are rejected out of hand, must be changed. The composition of the Party's National Executive Committee must be made much more truly representative of the three main elements of the movement (Parliamentary Party, Constituency Labour Parties and Trade Unions). We must proceed quickly to give effect to the 1982 Party Conference decision and clear out all those groups within the Party who are clearly at variance with its democratic aims and objectives. And we must drastically overhaul the Party's organizational and financial structure in order to stimulate the mobilization of public support.

Let nobody in the Labour Movement be in any doubt. The June 1983 General Election result puts a serious question-mark over whether the Party can survive as a credible political force in this country.

Margaret Thatcher and the Tories did not win the Election, so much as the Labour Party lost it. As many as 61 per cent of trade unionists did not vote Labour. The Tories even won more votes than Labour among skilled manual workers and only 44 per cent of the unemployed voted for the Party. Millions of ordinary people, whom Labour should be able to rely on for support, have deserted the Party and it will take a mammoth effort to recover so much lost ground quickly.

Both the industrial and political wings of the Labour Movement must take far more notice of what ordinary people are telling them. Neither unions nor party can afford to ignore the rank and file, the working-class voters, who no longer see Labour as their natural ally.

Time is not on Labour's side. There are real dangers that the hard Left will resume its advance inside the Movement in the next few years, winning back the ground it lost in 1981 and 1982. If this happens, the party will find it even harder than before to deny the allegation that it has become the prey of political extremism. Inevitably such a triumph for the hard Left will have a shattering effect on Labour's political position and push the party even further into third place over many parts of the country.

As for our trade unions my model of what can be done is West Germany, where the blueprint of industrial unionism was, in fact, drawn up by the British TUC after the defeat of Nazism. In November 1945 a delegation led by Will Lawther of the Mineworkers and Jack Tanner of the Engineers talked the German union leaders out of their original notion of having a single enormous union for all German workers, arguing that such an organization would be over-centralized, bureaucratic, and out of touch with the views of the rank and file.

The delegation emphasized the importance of rank-and-file involvement – still as essential now as it was then: 'The result of our experience, as representing the oldest trade union movement in the world, is that, important as organizational structure is, the strength of trade unionism depends largely upon the intelligence and enthusiasm of the members in the factories and pits and upon their active participation in all decisions.'

As an alternative to a single huge union, the TUC suggested that they create a trade union movement consisting, not of countless small unions, but of a number of unions each with 'complete autonomy over the industrial affairs of their members'. Above these bodies they recommended a confederation to be formed 'with authority to co-ordinate the policy of the unions'. This advice and frequent TUC visits over the next four years paved the way for the establishment of the West German DGB (Deutscher Gewerkschaftsbund) in October 1949, a more centralized and more powerful version of the TUC.

In essence this established the principles of industrial unionism, with one union representing all the people in one industry. But the Germans did not stop here. They were more concerned to take a positive role in economic planning than the TUC at that time, and were looking beyond the British system of joint consultation.

Their fundamental objectives, according to a British Government study of 1950, included 'the socialization of the basic industries, the establishment of a planned economy and the participation of the trade unions on the basis of equality in the management of industry and the shaping of economic policy'. While not all these aims were achieved, the West German unions have reached enough of their objectives to be able to play a positive role in the creation of a better society. This is especially due to the development of co-determination – union representatives on the boards of major companies with real power to help make decisions.

The prosperity of post-war West Germany shows the success of their approach. By having a small number of unions based on an industrial structure, the West German unions were able to exercise a considerable influence on economic policy and pay bargaining – and as a result both participated in and contributed to the boom in the country's economy. An important contributory factor is that they have enjoyed a centralized control that prevented inter-union rivalries and shop-floor fragmentation. The British TUC should enjoy similar power and authority.

But first a much more sensible and rational trade union structure needs to be created so we can put an end to the inter-union rivalries and incessant competition for new members that hamper our effectiveness. With fewer trade unions, based on different industrial interests, we could exercise far more influence with employers and Government. While the next few years will probably see further union mergers and amalgamations, present trends indicate that these will be of the wrong kind – conglomerates based on political attitudes rather than on industrial sense. For the union movement to be equipped for the next century it is up to the TUC itself to take a bold initiative and draw up a plan for a more coherent structure.

Mass unemployment, anti-union legislation, and the growth of new technologically based industries – all these factors are going to test the strength and ability of the trade unions to survive as robust defenders of working people. We need to gather what strength we have into a common strategy based on solidarity. I remain as convinced as ever that this will mean the inclusion of pay bargaining in a planned economy. And here a strong, well-organized trade union structure is essential, with industrial unions able to represent their members confidently in negotiations with government on the planning of our resources.

Under a further term of Mrs Thatcher the future of the railways looks bleak. We can expect to see more privatization and a starving of the investment needs of the industry. Serpell's recommendations may be implemented, and BR cut back to an Inter-City and South-East commuter service only. We are at a point where Britain has to decide whether it wants to have a good, modern nationwide network of railways, and if it does people will have to pay for it through taxes and subsidies. This, however, does not appear to be the intention of the Tory Government, and the alternative is for the railway network to decline and become ever more uncompetitive.

It is up to the railway unions to present and argue for policies which set out clearly how a modern railway system should be created so as to provide a service to the nation in the efficient movement of people and freight. This must include the acceptance of the new technologies and work practices which will make it possible. Despite the Thatcher Government's attitude to BR, the majority of the British people, including many Tory MPs, are favourably disposed towards railways, but it is up to those in the industry to prove that this really is the Age of the Train. This means starting again the process we began in 1981 of gaining the necessary commitment from each of the partners in the railways – the government, the British Railways Board and the unions. We must make public ownership work and this means a joint approach to solving the problems of the railways, a democratic bargain between each partner to synchronize efficiency and investment. The strikes of 1982 did grave damage and such nonsense must not be repeated; railway workers themselves will have to make sure they are not led by the nose into industrial disruption that only endangers the network and threatens their own job security.

In the end, it really comes down to what the rank-and-file workers want and are prepared to do to achieve their aims. The troubles of my years as General Secretary of the NUR taught me one lesson above all others: that unless people are vigilant and ready to act, a minority of political extremists will move in and seek to use trade unionism for their own destructive purposes. The same is as true of the Labour Party as of a trade union.

You can create the finest organization in the world on paper, but if people are not ready to exercise their rights, then democracy is in danger. I hope my friends in the broad Labour movement recognize that truth and act before it is too late. The price of failure is too terrible to contemplate, and it would do irreversible damage to all our hopes of making this country a better place to live in for working people and their families.

Index

McGahey, Mick (NUM) 44, 155
Macmillan, Harold 31
Maddock, Brian, 151, 152
manning levels 81, 82-3, 89-90, 166
Marsh, Sir Richard 32, 49
Militant Tendency 132, 134, 141, 142, 149-57
   158, 169
Milligan, John 148-9
Murray, Len 37-8, 41, 61, 85-6, 88, 96-7, 113,
   126, 127, 128-9

NALGO 39
National Economic Assessment 43-7
National Executive Committee (Labour
   Party) 23-4, 85, 114; elections to 158-61,
   162-3, 169, 171; and proscribed list 132-5,
   142; reform of 136-7, 138, 171
National Front 144-5
'No Rail Cuts' campaign 53, 55-6, 57-8
NUM see Gormley, Joe; Scargill, Arthur;
   Triple Alliance
NUPE 158
NUR conferences 19, 33; (1947) 18; (1975)
   82-3, 107, 131-2; (1976) 33-4, 56; (1978)
   34-6, 101, 131; (1979) 101; (1980) 126-7,
   132; (1981) 149, 150; (1982) 91-2, 94-5, 129,
   136-7, 159, 160, 164-7
NUR electoral system 25-6, 107-8, 156-7
NUR Executive Committee 19, 159, 160, 161,
   162-4, 167; reform of 99-101, 107-8; see also
   under Left, the hard
NUR modernization 99-111
NUR strike (1982) 88-93, 174
NUR training 101-3

Opportunity for Change 64

Parker, Sir Peter 49-51, 68-98 passim
Paynter, Will (NUM) 118
pay trains 60-65
Peel, Jack 118
Peyton, John 54
Phillips, Glyn (NALGO) 39
Policy for Transport 55
Prior, Jim 123
privatization 67, 109
public ownership 23, 48, 50, 51, 173

Rail Council 50-51
rail fares 52-3, 54
Rail Federation 125-9
rail pay crisis (1975) 27-32
Rail Policy 75-6
Railwaymen's Charter, The 66-72, 74, 76, 81
Raymond, Sir Stanley 49

Rees, Alun (NUR) 147
road lobby 49
Roberts, Bryn (NUPE) 118
Robinson, Derek 164
Rodgers, Bill 56, 57, 65, 131, 139

Sapper, Alan (ACTT) 96, 97
Scargill, Arthur (NUM) 123-5, 160
Serpell inquiry 55, 98, 173
Shore, Peter 56
Sirs, Bill (ISTC) 121-3
Social Contract 27, 28, 32-8, 40, 41, 43, 61, 132
Social Democrats 139, 140
Socialism 14, 35, 44, 125, 141-2
Socialist Workers' Party 151, 155
Stoneham, Ben 102, 103
Sunderland F.C. 17

Taaffe, Peter 150
TGWU 49, 117, 119, 120-21
Thatcher, Margaret 33, 42, 43, 44-5, 66-7, 95,
   96, 98, 121, 173
Towards a New Compact for Labour 135
Transport 2000 24-5, 52
Transport Act (1978) 57
Transport Review 106-7
Triple Alliance 121-5
TSSA 30, 70, 83; see also Rail Federation
TUC; and ASLEF 88, 96-8, 124; and
   'Concordat' 43, 45; and National Economic
   Assessment 45-7; reform of 117-21, 171-3;
   and Social Contract 32-4, 37-8; weakness of
   112-17; see also Murray, Len; West German
   trade union movement
Tuck, Russell 26, 84, 91, 159, 160, 162, 168
Turnock, Charlie 26, 59, 91, 111, 168

Unity House 103-5

Watford crisis summit (1980) 72-9
Weighell, Sidney
   birth 12; family 12-15; marriage 19, 21;
   NUR offices held 15-26; NUR resignation
   161-4; professional footballer 17; school 13,
   14; work experience 14-15; see also under
   Labour Party
West German trade union movement 117,
   171-3
What is the Future? 122
Whitehead, Philip 131
White Paper on transport (1977) 56-7
Williams, Ian 150, 152, 153, 154, 156
Wilson, (Sir) Harold 23, 25, 30-31, 45
Winter of Discontent 38-43
Woodcock, George 113